Yoga Nidra Meditation

Stress Management, Mental Health, and Inner Peace

Elianne Hartz

Introduction

Step into the enchanting realm of Yoga Nidra Meditation, where the gentle art of relaxation intertwines with the profound science of inner harmony.

Within the captivating pages of this book, prepare to embark on a voyage of self-discovery and empowerment, delving deep into the myriad benefits that Nidra Yoga offers for stress management, mental well-being, and the cultivation of enduring tranquility.

In a world where the pressures of modern life weigh heavily upon us, finding moments of solace amidst the chaos can seem like an impossible feat. Yet, nestled within the sanctuary of Nidra Yoga Meditation, lies a potent antidote to the burdens that burden our minds and bodies.

Here, within the digital pages of this transformative book, you will unearth a treasure trove of practical tools and profound insights to guide you through life's tumultuous seas with grace and resilience.

From expertly crafted relaxation techniques to mindfulness practices that transcend the ordinary, each chapter is meticulously designed to illuminate a path towards greater well-being and vitality.

Whether you find yourself grappling with the relentless grip of stress, yearning for a deeper connection with your inner self, or simply longing for a moment of peace amidst the bustling chaos of everyday life, Nidra Yoga Meditation beckons, offering the promise of unlocking your boundless potential.

So, dear reader, join us as we embark upon an odyssey into the transformative depths of Nidra Yoga Meditation. Together, let us navigate the winding trails towards a life imbued with balance, clarity, and profound inner peace. The adventure awaits, and the journey begins now.

Chapter 1: The Power of Nidra Yoga Meditation

Experience the profound tranquility of Nidra Yoga Meditation, also known as Yoga Nidra or Yogic Sleep. Rooted in ancient wisdom, this practice seamlessly blends the benefits of yoga and meditation to induce deep relaxation, alleviate stress, and nurture holistic well-being.

Within the serenity of Nidra Yoga Meditation, practitioners embark on a guided journey towards inner peace. Comfortably reclined, they surrender to the soothing voice of a teacher, navigating through a sequence of relaxation techniques.

Central to its essence is the profound dual relaxation—physical and mental—that Nidra Yoga Meditation instills. Through mindful breathwork, thorough body scans, and vivid visualizations, it fosters a tangible reduction in stress and anxiety, fostering restorative sleep and holistic balance. Particularly poignant is its efficacy in aiding those grappling with insomnia, chronic stress, or anxiety disorders.

Yet, beyond mere relaxation lies the gateway to the subconscious mind. Within the depths of deep relaxation, participants unearth their innermost thoughts, emotions, and beliefs. This introspective journey proves invaluable for those seeking positive transformation, offering a platform to unearth and liberate from detrimental patterns hindering personal growth.

Beyond its profound impact on relaxation and inner peace, Nidra Yoga Meditation extends its benefits to physical well-being. Scientifically proven, this practice demonstrates remarkable effects in reducing blood pressure, enhancing immune function, and fostering overall bodily health. By mitigating stress and inducing relaxation, it serves as a proactive measure against chronic ailments like heart disease, diabetes, and obesity.

Central to the ethos of Nidra Yoga Meditation is the concept of sankalpa, or intention setting. Within the meditation, participants are urged to cultivate positive intentions or aspirations, which they reverberate throughout the session. This intentional focus empowers individuals to channel their energies towards personal growth, health, relationships, or career aspirations.

In its entirety, Nidra Yoga Meditation emerges as a potent tool for deep relaxation, stress alleviation, and holistic well-being. Seamlessly integrating the virtues of yoga and meditation, it offers a comprehensive approach to wellness accessible to individuals of diverse ages and fitness levels. Whether seeking stress reduction, improved sleep, or personal evolution, Nidra Yoga Meditation serves as a guiding light towards a harmonious and fulfilling existence.

Understanding the Practice of Nidra Yoga

Discover the transformative power of Nidra Yoga, often dubbed as Yogic Sleep, a dynamic fusion of meditation, relaxation, and mindfulness aimed at fostering deep relaxation and renewal.

This age-old practice has witnessed a surge in popularity as more individuals seek avenues to alleviate stress, enrich sleep quality, and nurture holistic well-being.

Central to the practice of Nidra Yoga is the art of reclining in a comfortable posture and embarking on a guided journey through a repertoire of relaxation techniques. The ultimate aim is to immerse oneself in a profound state of relaxation while maintaining consciousness and awareness of the present moment—a state often likened to the threshold between wakefulness and sleep.

An integral component of Nidra Yoga is the concept of sankalpa, or intention, which is seeded at the onset of the practice. This intention serves as a beacon, illuminating the path towards desired outcomes such as enhanced health, abundance, or tranquility.

Through repetitive reinforcement during the session, one can sow the seeds of positive transformation within the depths of the subconscious mind, catalyzing the realization of aspirations in the tangible realm.

An integral component of Nidra Yoga lies in its profound emphasis on breathwork. Through mindful attention to the breath and the application of specific breathing techniques, one can usher in a cascade of benefits—calming the mind, soothing the body, and descending into a realm of profound relaxation.

This deliberate focus on the breath acts as a conduit for quieting the mind and unraveling bodily tension, paving the way for an exquisite sense of serenity and tranquility.

Within the realm of Nidra Yoga, practitioners often embark on a journey of body scanning, meticulously directing attention to each part of the body while consciously ushering in relaxation. This deliberate process aids in the dissolution of tension and stress, fostering a profound state of rejuvenation and inner calm.

By bestowing awareness upon every corner of the body and intentionally releasing accumulated tension, one initiates a transformative journey toward physical, mental, and emotional healing.

Nidra Yoga stands as a practice accessible to individuals of all ages and fitness levels, extending its therapeutic embrace to those grappling with stress, anxiety, insomnia, and assorted mental health challenges.

Through consistent engagement with Nidra Yoga, one can forge pathways to stress reduction, enhanced sleep quality, and holistic well-being.

Moreover, the practice holds promise in enhancing cognitive faculties such as focus, concentration, and creative prowess, rendering it an invaluable asset for students, athletes, and professionals alike.

At the heart of Nidra Yoga lies its profound capacity to induce deep relaxation and renewal. Immersed in the embrace of yogic slumber, practitioners shed layers of tension and stress, granting passage to a realm suffused with tranquility and serenity. This profound relaxation serves as a salve, alleviating anxiety, enhancing sleep quality, and nurturing holistic well-being.

Moreover, Nidra Yoga serves as a potent catalyst for sharpening mental acuity and fostering unwavering focus. Quieting the incessant chatter of the mind and liberating the body from its burdens, it empowers individuals to hone their concentration and clarity of thought.

Such cognitive enhancement proves invaluable for students, professionals, and individuals striving for peak performance in their daily endeavors.

Furthermore, the therapeutic benefits of Nidra Yoga extend far beyond the confines of the physical realm, permeating into the realms of mental and emotional healing.

By liberating the body from the shackles of tension and stress, practitioners pave the way for profound healing and equilibrium. This holistic approach not only diminishes pain and enhances circulation but also fosters a profound sense of vitality and wholeness, uplifting the spirit and fortifying overall health and well-being.

Nidra Yoga serves as a gateway to liberation on mental and emotional planes, offering a pathway to untangle negative thought patterns and emotions, thus ushering in profound peace and clarity. Delving into deep relaxation, practitioners effortlessly shed the burdens of stress, anxiety, and other psychological constraints, paving the way for a harmonious equilibrium.

Beyond its tangible benefits for physical, mental, and emotional well-being, Nidra Yoga emerges as a catalyst for spiritual evolution and heightened awareness.

Through introspection and intention setting, individuals forge a connection with their inner essence, aligning with their highest aspirations and catalyzing their manifestation in the tangible realm. This alignment fosters a life of purpose and fulfillment, guided by authentic desires and intentions.

In essence, Nidra Yoga stands as a potent practice offering multifaceted benefits, spanning the realms of physical rejuvenation, mental clarity, emotional equilibrium, and spiritual growth. Through the gateway of deep relaxation and yogic slumber, practitioners unlock the gates to peace and tranquility, ushering in a life marked by fulfillment and balance.

Whether embarking on the yoga journey as a novice or seasoned practitioner, Nidra Yoga remains an invaluable tool for navigating the currents of existence with grace and harmony.

Embracing Stillness and Tranquility

Amidst the relentless hustle of modern life, finding moments of stillness and tranquility poses a formidable challenge. Amidst the ceaseless barrage of distractions and an ever-expanding agenda, carving out space to simply breathe can seem like an unattainable luxury.

Yet, amidst this chaos, the embrace of stillness and tranquility emerges as not merely a luxury, but a vital necessity for our holistic well-being.

In a world perpetually inundating us with stimuli and information overload, the art of stillness grants us an invaluable opportunity to recharge and recalibrate. It offers a sanctuary from the cacophony of external chaos, affording us a rare chance to commune with our inner selves.

The benefits of embracing stillness and tranquility extend far beyond mere relaxation; they permeate every facet of our being, nurturing our mental, emotional, and physical health.

By quieting the incessant chatter of the mind, we unlock the door to a realm of reduced stress and anxiety, heightened focus and creativity, and an overarching sense of inner serenity and fulfillment. Through this deliberate cultivation of presence, we gain clarity and perspective, illuminating the path to a more meaningful existence.

Fortunately, there exist myriad avenues through which we can integrate stillness and tranquility into our daily lives. Among these, mindfulness meditation stands out as a simple yet potent practice.

 By immersing ourselves in the present moment and observing our thoughts and feelings with gentle curiosity, we cultivate a state of mindful awareness that transcends the chaos of the external world, anchoring us in a profound sense of inner peace and tranquility.

Venturing into nature offers a profound avenue for embracing stillness and tranquility. Immersed in the natural world, we find solace for our mental and emotional well-being.

The sights, sounds, and fragrances of nature ground us, fostering a profound sense of connection to the world around us. Whether wandering through a verdant park, lingering by a tranquil lake, or marveling at the celestial canopy, communing with nature serves as a potent catalyst for discovering inner peace and tranquility.

Moreover, the ancient practices of yoga and tai chi stand as venerable gateways to cultivating stillness and tranquility. Through gentle movements harmonized with breath awareness, these disciplines orchestrate a symphony of relaxation and inner harmony.

Centering our attention on the interplay of body and breath, we quiet the tumult of the mind, ushering in a state of profound equilibrium and balance.

Incorporating moments of stillness and tranquility into our daily rhythm bears transformative potential for our overall well-being.

Whether it's the simple act of taking deep breaths at the dawn of a new day, pausing for a moment of silence before partaking in a meal, or carving out time for quiet reflection or prayer, these intentional interludes nourish the soul and replenish the spirit, infusing our lives with a sense of peace and serenity amidst the tumult of modern existence.

Embracing stillness and tranquility is a continual voyage, not a fixed destination. It demands patience and dedication to nurture a sanctuary of inner peace and serenity.

Amidst the tumult of life, there will be days when finding stillness seems an insurmountable task. Yet, by steadfastly committing to carve out moments of quiet reflection, we gradually assimilate stillness and tranquility into the fabric of our existence.

In essence, embracing stillness and tranquility is an indispensable cornerstone of holistic well-being. In a world perpetually ensnared in the frenzy of activity, the art of stillness offers a sanctuary wherein we can recharge, recalibrate, and rediscover our essence.

Through the infusion of mindfulness meditation, communing with nature, the graceful movements of yoga and tai chi, and punctuating our routines with moments of quietude, we forge a pathway towards inner peace and tranquility that permeates every facet of our lives.

So, amidst the chaos, pause, take a deep breath, and embrace the enduring tranquility that resides within.

Chapter 2: Harnessing the Healing Energy of Nidra

Delve into the realm of Nidra, often referred to as yogic sleep, where the profound synergy of deep relaxation and meditation converge to unleash the body's innate healing prowess.

This timeless practice, revered through the ages, serves as a conduit for fostering holistic well-being across the physical, mental, and emotional spectrums. Through the gentle embrace of deep relaxation, practitioners embark on a journey to unlock the body's reservoir of healing energies, ushering in a tapestry of health and vitality.

Rooted in Sanskrit, "Nidra" translates to "sleep" in English, yet its essence transcends mere slumber. Rather, Nidra beckons individuals to traverse the realms of consciousness while submerged in a profound state of relaxation.

Guided through a series of meticulously crafted relaxation techniques, practitioners shed layers of tension, quiet the cacophony of the mind, and immerse themselves in a sanctuary of tranquility.

Within this cocoon of deep relaxation, the body finds solace, embarking on a voyage of healing and rejuvenation that reverberates throughout the entire being, nurturing overall health and well-being.

Foremost among the myriad gifts of Nidra is its unparalleled ability to instill deep relaxation and alleviate the burdens of stress. In the frenetic pace of modern life, stress emerges as a ubiquitous affliction, casting a shadow over both physical and mental well-being.

Through regular engagement with Nidra, individuals glean the art of releasing tension and stress, thereby cultivating a sanctuary of calm and serenity within. This newfound equilibrium serves as a potent antidote to anxiety, fostering restful sleep and fostering a flourishing sense of overall well-being.

Beyond its prowess in stress reduction, Nidra extends its therapeutic embrace to the realm of sleep enhancement. For many, the elusive quest for restful slumber proves a daunting challenge, as insomnia and sleep disturbances cast a pall over their well-being. Yet, by embracing Nidra before bedtime, individuals unlock the key to relaxation, paving the way for a serene journey into the realm of sleep.

The fusion of deep relaxation and meditative techniques inherent in Nidra serves to quiet the mind, fostering a sanctuary of peace and tranquility conducive to undisturbed sleep throughout the night.

Moreover, Nidra emerges as a potent catalyst for facilitating healing and rejuvenation within the body's intricate tapestry. Immersed in the depths of profound relaxation, the body shifts its focus towards cellular repair and restoration.

This innate healing process, orchestrated by the restorative energies of Nidra, fortifies the immune system, quells inflammation, and nurtures overall health and vitality.

Through harnessing the healing energies of Nidra, individuals embolden their body's innate capacity for rejuvenation, cultivating a harmonious state of optimal health and wellness.

In tandem with its physical benefits, Nidra exerts a profound influence on mental and emotional well-being. The fusion of deep relaxation and meditative practices inherent in Nidra serves as a balm for the restless mind, assuaging anxiety and fostering a profound sense of inner tranquility.

This transformative journey equips individuals with the tools to navigate the vicissitudes of life with grace and resilience, fostering emotional well-being and enhancing overall mental health.

Through regular engagement with Nidra, individuals cultivate a steadfast foundation of mindfulness and self-awareness, empowering them to navigate life's challenges with equanimity and fortitude.

At the heart of Nidra lies the profound principle of sankalpa—an affirmative intention set at the outset of each session. Anchored in positivity, this intention becomes a beacon guiding practitioners towards transformative change.

By steadfastly focusing on a positive sankalpa during Nidra practice, individuals harness the boundless power of their minds to sculpt a reality aligned with their deepest aspirations.

In this sacred space, limiting beliefs dissolve, fostering a profound sense of self-love, acceptance, and the realization of dreams. Through the symbiotic dance of sankalpa and Nidra, individuals unearth their inner wisdom, catalyzing a cascade of positive transformation in their lives.

Indeed, Nidra emerges as a potent elixir, weaving together the threads of deep relaxation and meditation to orchestrate a symphony of healing. Immersed in the embrace of profound relaxation, practitioners unlock the gateways to physical, mental, and emotional well-being.

Stress ebbs away, sleep deepens, and the body's innate healing mechanisms are activated. Augmented by the steadfast guidance of a positive intention, Nidra becomes a conduit for mindfulness and self-awareness, nurturing emotional resilience and fortifying overall well-being.

Embracing the healing currents of Nidra, individuals embark on a journey towards balance, peace, and fulfillment, sculpting a life imbued with harmony and serenity.

Cultivating Inner
Peace through Nidra

In the whirlwind of modern life, the quest for inner peace and serenity remains a constant pursuit for many. Amidst this quest, Yoga Nidra emerges as a beacon of tranquility, offering a sanctuary of calm amidst the chaos.

Rooted in ancient tradition, this practice, also known as yogic sleep, has surged in popularity as seekers yearn for profound relaxation and heightened awareness. Through the gentle guidance of Yoga Nidra, individuals embark on a transformative journey towards inner harmony, stress reduction, and holistic well-being.

What is Yoga Nidra?

Yoga Nidra traces its origins to the ancient Indian tradition of yoga, offering a pathway to deep relaxation and heightened consciousness. The practice unfolds as individuals recline in comfort, guided through a tapestry of meditation techniques designed to usher them into a realm of profound tranquility while retaining a gentle thread of awareness.

Within the sacred space of a Yoga Nidra session, practitioners navigate a labyrinth of body scans, breath awareness, visualizations, and affirmations. Each technique serves as a conduit for releasing tension, quieting the mind, and nurturing inner peace.

Benefits of Yoga Nidra

The benefits of regular Yoga Nidra practice are manifold, yielding a rich tapestry of holistic well-being:

1. Stress Reduction: At its core, Yoga Nidra excels in alleviating stress and anxiety. By immersing in deep relaxation, practitioners shed the burdens of tension, paving the way for a profound sense of tranquility and equilibrium.

2. Restorative Sleep: Amidst the struggle with insomnia and related sleep disorders, Yoga Nidra emerges as a soothing remedy, enhancing the quality of sleep and facilitating a more rejuvenating slumber.

3. Heightened Awareness: Within the gentle embrace of Yoga Nidra, individuals embark on a journey towards heightened self-awareness and mindfulness. By anchoring themselves in the present moment and nurturing inner tranquility, practitioners develop a profound attunement to their thoughts, emotions, and actions.

4. Unleashed Creativity: Delving into the depths of deep relaxation, Yoga Nidra unlocks the floodgates of creativity and problem-solving prowess. As practitioners surrender to the subconscious realm, they unearth novel ideas and insights, fostering a fertile ground for innovation.

5. Emotional Rejuvenation: Beneath the surface, many carry the weight of emotional scars and traumas that cast a shadow over their well-being.

Through the healing currents of Yoga Nidra, individuals embark on a journey of emotional release and renewal, shedding the shackles of negativity and cultivating a profound sense of emotional harmony and well-being.

Mastering the art of Yoga Nidra is within reach for everyone, irrespective of age or fitness level. Begin by finding a tranquil space where interruptions are unlikely, laying down comfortably—perhaps on a yoga mat or a cozy blanket.

Close your eyes and attune your focus to your breath, inhaling and exhaling deeply to initiate relaxation. Progress by mentally scanning your body from head to toe, noting areas of tension or discomfort.

Embark on a guided meditation or visualization, either through a recording or self-guided. Maintain a gentle awareness of your breath throughout, allowing each technique to deepen your state of relaxation while staying conscious and present.

In your Yoga Nidra journey, embrace a state of surrender, releasing expectations and judgments. Simply allow yourself to bask in the present moment, absorbing the tranquility it offers. Over time and consistent practice, revel in the benefits of heightened inner peace, diminished stress, and an enhanced sense of well-being.

Tips for Cultivating Inner Peace through Nidra

1. Dedicate Time for Practice: Consistency is key in reaping the rewards of Yoga Nidra. Allocate a regular slot in your daily routine—be it morning, afternoon, or evening—and honor it with commitment.

2. Craft a Serene Ambiance: Cultivate an environment conducive to tranquility. Seek out a quiet, cozy space and consider enhancing it with soft lighting, soothing music, or fragrant candles to amplify the calming effect.

3. Embrace Openness: Approach your practice with a spirit of openness and receptivity. Release any preconceived notions and surrender to the unfolding experience, allowing it to unfold naturally.

4. Practice Self-Compassion: Be kind and gentle with yourself throughout your Yoga Nidra journey. If distractions arise or your mind wanders, extend compassion to yourself and gently guide your focus back to the breath, nurturing a sense of inner peace and acceptance.

A Path to Self-Discovery

Exploring the profound realms of Nidra Yoga unveils a transformative journey towards self-discovery and inner peace. Delve into the origins, benefits, and transformative potential of this ancient practice as we embark on a voyage of self-exploration.

Rooted in the annals of ancient India, Nidra Yoga emerges as a beacon of guided meditation, facilitating a harmonious convergence of deep relaxation and heightened consciousness.

Envisioned as a tapestry of serenity, practitioners recline in comfort, guided by the gentle prompts of a seasoned instructor or recorded session. Through a symphony of guided visualizations, body scans, and breath awareness techniques, individuals traverse the labyrinthine pathways of their subconscious, unraveling the mysteries of their inner landscape.

Foremost among the myriad benefits of Nidra Yoga is its profound capacity to dissolve the shackles of stress and tension ensnaring body and mind. Immersed in the sanctuary of deep relaxation, practitioners relinquish the burdens of worry and anxiety, paving the way for restorative sleep, diminished anxiety, and an overarching sense of well-being.

Beyond its prowess in stress reduction, Nidra Yoga emerges as a potent catalyst for self-discovery. Within the recesses of the subconscious, practitioners unearth the hidden gems of beliefs, fears, and desires that silently orchestrate the symphony of their lives.

Illuminated by the beacon of awareness, individuals embark on a journey of introspection and transformation, aligning with their authentic selves and charting a course towards profound fulfillment and self-realization.

Engaging in consistent Nidra Yoga sessions facilitates the nurturing of heightened self-awareness and self-compassion. Through this practice, individuals forge a profound connection with their inner wisdom and intuition, illuminating the path towards understanding their life purpose and core values.

Decisions made in alignment with their authentic selves breed a profound sense of fulfillment, happiness, and interconnectedness with the world.

A distinctive facet of Nidra Yoga lies in its ability to penetrate the depths of the subconscious, where entrenched beliefs and emotions lie dormant. By conscientiously engaging with the subconscious realm, practitioners embark on a journey of reprogramming, shedding antiquated patterns and embracing empowering beliefs conducive to personal growth and transformation.

This journey heralds profound shifts in consciousness, fostering a newfound sense of liberation and empowerment.

In tandem with its psychological benefits, Nidra Yoga bestows a plethora of physical advantages. Plunging into deep relaxation induces a lowering of heart rate, reduction in blood pressure, and enhancement of circulation. These physiological adjustments fortify the immune system, quell inflammation, and foster holistic well-being.

Indeed, Nidra Yoga emerges as a potent conduit for profound self-discovery and metamorphosis. By delving into the depths of relaxation and accessing the subconscious reservoirs, practitioners unearth latent beliefs and emotions, liberate themselves from stress and tension, and nurture an expansive sense of self-awareness and self-compassion.

 Through dedicated practice, individuals harmonize with their authentic selves, sculpting a life attuned to their deepest values and aspirations.

For those intrigued by the transformative potential of Nidra Yoga, a wealth of resources awaits exploration. Many yoga studios offer classes, workshops, and retreats dedicated to Nidra Yoga, fostering a nurturing and supportive environment for practice.

Additionally, a myriad of books, online courses, and recordings extend guidance, enabling practitioners to embark on their journey from the comfort of home.

Embarking on your Nidra Yoga journey beckons for an open mind and a spirit of curiosity. Surrender yourself to the experience, embracing the trust that each practice session is a step towards profound self-discovery and inner peace. Through commitment and perseverance, Nidra Yoga unfurls as a transformative ally, nurturing growth and guiding you towards a life brimming with authenticity and fulfillment.

Chapter 3: The Transformative Effects of Nidra Meditation

Nidra meditation, also known as yoga nidra or yogic sleep, stands as a potent and increasingly popular practice, steeped in ancient wisdom yet resonating powerfully in our modern world.

This guided meditation technique beckons practitioners into a state of profound relaxation while retaining consciousness, offering transformative effects that ripple through both mind and body.

Foremost among the myriad benefits of nidra meditation is its remarkable capacity to alleviate stress and anxiety. In the relentless hustle of contemporary life, stressors abound, taxing mental and physical well-being.

Nidra meditation serves as a sanctuary, a haven where practitioners can unwind, releasing tension and shedding worries. Through this deep relaxation, individuals find solace and tranquility, fostering a sense of peace that permeates their daily existence.

Moreover, nidra meditation holds promise in improving sleep quality—a boon for many grappling with insomnia and related disorders. By embracing nidra meditation as a regular practice, individuals pave the way for their minds and bodies to sink into profound relaxation.

This facilitates easier transitions into slumber and sustains restful sleep throughout the night, nurturing a sense of renewal upon waking.

In essence, nidra meditation emerges as a beacon of serenity and restoration, offering respite from the tumult of modern life. Its profound effects ripple through the fabric of existence, guiding practitioners towards a state of profound well-being and vitality.

Moreover, nidra meditation unfolds as a powerful ally in nurturing mental health. Research indicates that regular engagement in nidra meditation yields notable reductions in symptoms of depression and anxiety, while concurrently enhancing overall mental well-being.

As practitioners immerse themselves in a state of deep relaxation and attune to the present moment, they glean clarity and perspective, equipping them with enhanced coping mechanisms to navigate life's trials and tribulations.

This fosters emotional equilibrium and resilience, fostering a heightened sense of happiness and well-being.

Furthermore, nidra meditation exerts a transformative influence by igniting creativity and intuition. Through deep relaxation, individuals unlock the gateway to their subconscious mind, tapping into a wellspring of inner wisdom and creativity.

This journey yields fresh insights, ideas, and inspiration, transcending creative impasses. Indeed, artists, writers, and creatives across various disciplines acclaim nidra meditation as a potent catalyst for unlocking their creative potential and surmounting artistic barriers.

Moreover, nidra meditation extends its profound influence to physical health. Delving into a state of deep relaxation, practitioners alleviate bodily tension, bolster circulation, and foster cellular rejuvenation and healing.

This fosters a heightened sense of vitality and well-being while mitigating the risk of chronic ailments such as heart disease, diabetes, and obesity. Furthermore, nidra meditation emerges as a potent ally in fortifying the immune system, curbing inflammation, and nurturing overall health and longevity.

In sum, the transformative potential of nidra meditation spans a multitude of dimensions. Through consistent engagement in this guided meditation practice, individuals unlock a pathway to heightened peace, relaxation, and well-being.

Moreover, they reap the rewards of improved mental, emotional, and physical health. Whether seeking to alleviate stress, enhance sleep quality, unleash creativity, or fortify overall health and well-being, nidra meditation stands as a invaluable resource for realizing one's aspirations and fostering a life of fulfillment and equilibrium.

Finding Balance and Harmony with Nidra

Finding balance and harmony in life is a goal that many people strive for. In today's fast-paced world, it can be challenging to find time for yourself and to focus on your own well-being. However, one practice that can help you achieve balance and harmony in your life is yoga nidra.

Yoga nidra, also known as yogic sleep, is a form of guided meditation that allows you to enter a state of deep relaxation while remaining conscious.

It is a powerful practice that can help you reduce stress, improve sleep, and increase self-awareness. By incorporating yoga nidra into your daily routine, you can find greater balance and harmony in all aspects of your life.

One of the key benefits of yoga nidra is its ability to help you relax and reduce stress. In today's busy world, stress is a common problem that can have a negative impact on your physical and mental health.

By practicing yoga nidra regularly, you can release tension from your body and mind, allowing you to feel more relaxed and at ease.

During a yoga nidra session, you will be guided through a series of relaxation techniques that help you enter a state of deep relaxation. By focusing on your breath and body sensations, you can let go of any stress or tension that you may be holding onto. This can help you feel more calm and centered, even in the midst of a hectic day.

In addition to reducing stress, yoga nidra can also help improve your sleep. Many people struggle with insomnia or other sleep disorders, which can have a negative impact on their overall well-being.

By practicing yoga nidra before bed, you can relax your body and mind, making it easier to fall asleep and stay asleep throughout the night.

Yoga nidra can also help you increase self-awareness and mindfulness. By tuning into your body and breath during a yoga nidra session, you can become more aware of your thoughts and emotions.

This increased self- awareness can help you make better choices and decisions in your daily life, leading to greater balance and harmony.

To practice yoga nidra, all you need is a quiet space where you can lie down comfortably. You can find guided yoga nidra sessions online or attend a class at a local yoga studio.

During a yoga nidra session, you will be guided through a series of relaxation techniques, such as body scanning, breath awareness, and visualization. These techniques can help you relax your body and mind, allowing you to enter a state of deep relaxation.

As you practice yoga nidra regularly, you may start to notice positive changes in your life. You may feel more relaxed and at ease, even in stressful situations.

You may also notice improvements in your sleep and overall well- being. By finding balance and harmony through yoga nidra, you can live a more fulfilling and joyful life.

In conclusion, yoga nidra is a powerful practice that can help you find balance and harmony in your life. By reducing stress, improving sleep, and increasing self-awareness, yoga nidra can have a positive impact on your physical and mental health.

If you are looking to find greater balance and harmony in your life, consider incorporating yoga nidra into your daily routine. With regular practice, you can experience the many benefits of this transformative practice and live a more peaceful and fulfilling life.

Yoga for Stress
Relief and Relaxation

Nidra Yoga, also referred to as Yoga Nidra or Yogic Sleep, stands as a potent method for inducing profound relaxation and alleviating stress.

Rooted in ancient yogic tradition, this guided meditation practice enables participants to enter a state akin to conscious relaxation, resembling deep sleep.

Through Nidra Yoga, individuals unlock avenues to experience deep physical, mental, and emotional relaxation, fostering a sense of renewal and holistic well-being.

Central to the efficacy of Nidra Yoga is its capacity to activate the parasympathetic nervous system, recognized as the "rest and digest" response.

In contrast to the sympathetic nervous system's role in triggering the body's stress-induced "fight or flight" reaction, stimulating the parasympathetic system via Nidra Yoga prompts a decrease in heart rate, a reduction in blood pressure, and a serene state of mind, fostering profound relaxation and tranquility.

A paramount advantage of Nidra Yoga lies in its capability to facilitate the release of tension and stress from both the body and mind. Through guided relaxation techniques, practitioners shed physical and mental strains, ushering in a profound sense of calmness and relaxation. This proves especially beneficial for individuals grappling with chronic stress, anxiety, or insomnia, as Nidra Yoga serves to quiet the mind and nurture inner peace.

Beyond stress relief, Nidra Yoga emerges as a potent instrument for nurturing overall health and well-being. Studies have demonstrated its efficacy in enhancing sleep quality, bolstering immune function, and refining cognitive abilities.

By fostering deep relaxation and mitigating stress levels, Nidra Yoga empowers individuals to feel more invigorated, focused, and emotionally balanced.

Nidra Yoga's effectiveness in alleviating stress and inducing relaxation stems from its multifaceted approach to the mind and body.

Through a series of guided relaxation techniques, this practice targets tension release in the physical body, calming of the mind, and fostering inner peace.

By honing attention on the breath, bodily sensations, and mental imagery, practitioners delve into a profound state of relaxation, paving the way for healing and revitalization.

To engage in Nidra Yoga for stress relief and relaxation, it's essential to carve out a serene and cozy space conducive to unwinding without disturbances.

Whether on a yoga mat or a soft surface like a bed or couch, ensuring comfort is key. Employing a blanket or cushion for support and warmth is advisable for a comfortable experience.

Commence your Nidra Yoga practice by reclining on your back, limbs comfortably extended alongside your body. Close your eyes, inhaling deeply to center yourself and release bodily tension with each exhale. Tune into any areas of tightness or stress within your body, consciously letting go as you exhale.

Once a sense of relaxation permeates, shift your focus to your breath. Observe its natural ebb and flow, attuning to its rhythm as it traverses your body.

Progressively direct your awareness from your toes to your head, channeling relaxation and healing energy with each inhalation and exhalation. Visualize tension dissolving with each breath, fostering a state of profound tranquility and renewal.

As you maintain focus on your breath and bodily sensations, you may observe thoughts or emotions emerging in your mind.

Rather than becoming entangled in these thoughts, simply acknowledge them and let them pass, redirecting your attention to your breath and bodily sensations. Through this present awareness, you can deepen your relaxation and enter a state of profound inner tranquility.

Throughout the Nidra Yoga session, the guided meditation will further facilitate relaxation and release any lingering tension or stress.

The instructor will lead you through visualizations and affirmations crafted to foster relaxation, healing, and positive transformation. Surrendering to the guidance, you can immerse yourself in profound relaxation and stress relief.

Upon concluding the Nidra Yoga practice, take a moment to rest and absorb the experience. Gently transition to a seated position, taking deep breaths to reawaken your body and mind.

Reflect on the aftermath of the practice—do you sense increased relaxation, centeredness, and peace? Acknowledge any shifts in your physical, mental, or emotional state, allowing yourself to bask in the practice's benefits.

Integrating Nidra Yoga into your daily regimen can profoundly diminish stress, elevate relaxation, and enrich overall well-being. Devoting mere minutes each day to this practice can yield profound benefits for your mind, body, and soul.

Chapter 4: Unlocking the Secrets of Nidra Meditation

Nidra meditation, also known as Yoga Nidra, stands as a profound and transformative practice that has garnered increased attention in recent times.

Rooted in ancient traditions, this form of meditation is renowned for inducing profound relaxation, facilitating healing, and nurturing self-discovery. In this discourse, we delve into the essence of Nidra meditation and unveil how you can unlock its myriad benefits in your personal journey.

Understanding Nidra Meditation:

Nidra meditation constitutes a guided practice that intertwines deep relaxation with conscious awareness. Originating from the Sanskrit term "Nidra," meaning sleep, this practice orchestrates a state akin to sleep, albeit with full consciousness and awareness intact.

In Nidra meditation, individuals recline in a comfortable posture, shut their eyes, and engage with a guided meditation that leads them through a series of body scans, visualizations, and affirmations.

Crafted to foster deep relaxation and inner tranquility, this practice also empowers practitioners to delve into the subconscious mind, addressing emotional or mental barriers along the way.

Unveiling the Secrets of Nidra Meditation:

Nidra meditation harbors potent secrets that unfold through regular practice, enriching the lives of those who embrace it. Here, we illuminate some of these secrets and unveil how you can harness its full potential:

1. Profound Relaxation: At the heart of Nidra meditation lies its capacity to usher individuals into a realm of profound relaxation. By gently guiding practitioners into a state of deep repose, Nidra meditation mitigates stress, anxiety, and bodily tension. This holistic relaxation imparts a spectrum of benefits, including enhanced sleep quality, augmented vitality, and an amplified sense of serenity and tranquility.

1. **Healing:** Nidra meditation is renowned for its profound healing potential. By delving into the subconscious mind during meditation, practitioners can address emotional and mental barriers that may manifest as physical or emotional pain. This journey fosters inner peace, healing, and a sense of completeness.

2. **Self-Discovery:** Nidra meditation serves as a potent catalyst for self-discovery and personal evolution. By tapping into the subconscious realm during meditation, individuals unlock insights into their thoughts, emotions, and beliefs. This process facilitates a deeper

understanding of oneself, motivations, and aspirations, fostering enhanced self-awareness and personal growth.

3. **Stress Relief:** Amidst the hustle and bustle of modern life, Nidra meditation emerges as a valuable antidote to stress. Regular practice enables practitioners to attain profound relaxation, releasing tension and worry to cultivate inner calm and tranquility. This equips individuals with the tools to navigate stress, anxiety, and overwhelm, nurturing holistic well-being.

4. **Improved Sleep:** Nidra meditation is renowned for its efficacy in enhancing sleep quality. By integrating Nidra meditation into bedtime routines, individuals unwind both body and mind, shedding stress and tension to prepare for a restful night's sleep. This paves the way for easier sleep onset, prolonged rest, and waking up feeling refreshed and revitalized.

How to Practice Nidra Meditation:

1. **Find a Quiet and Comfortable Space:** Create a serene environment conducive to meditation, where you can recline and unwind without interruptions.

2. **Set an Intention:** Prior to commencing your practice, establish a clear intention, focusing on relaxation, healing, or self-discovery.

3. **Follow a Guided Meditation:** Utilize guided Nidra meditation sessions to navigate body scans, visualizations, and affirmations tailored to your needs.

4. **Relax and Let Go:** Surrender to the meditation, releasing tension, stress, and worry to immerse yourself in deep relaxation and inner peace.

5. **Stay Present and Aware:** Remain attuned to your experience, observing thoughts, emotions, and sensations with non-judgmental awareness. Allow them to arise and dissipate naturally as you delve deeper into your practice.

Healing the Mind, Body
and Spirit with Nidra

In today's fast-paced world, many of us are constantly on the go, juggling work, family, and social commitments. This hectic lifestyle can take a toll on our mental, physical, and spiritual well-being.

It's important to take time for ourselves to relax, recharge, and heal. One powerful tool for healing the mind, body, and spirit is the practice of Yoga Nidra.

Yoga Nidra, also known as yogic sleep, is a form of guided meditation that allows the practitioner to enter a state of deep relaxation while remaining fully conscious. It is a systematic method of inducing complete physical, mental, and emotional relaxation.

The practice involves lying down in a comfortable position and following the instructions of a trained facilitator as they guide you through a series of relaxation techniques.

The benefits of Yoga Nidra are numerous and profound. It can help to reduce stress, anxiety, and depression, improve sleep quality, boost immune function, increase focus and concentration, and enhance overall well-being. The practice has been used for centuries in traditional Indian medicine as a powerful tool for healing and transformation.

Healing the Mind

Our minds are constantly bombarded with thoughts, worries, and distractions. This can lead to mental fatigue, anxiety, and overwhelm.

Yoga Nidra offers a way to quiet the mind and find inner peace. By following the guided instructions and focusing on the present moment, we can release mental tension and reduce the chatter of the mind.

Yoga Nidra can help to reprogram negative thought patterns and beliefs, allowing us to cultivate a more positive and empowering mindset.

The practice can also help to increase self-awareness and mindfulness, enabling us to observe our thoughts and emotions without judgment. This can lead to greater clarity, insight, and emotional resilience.

Healing the Body

Our bodies are often neglected in our busy lives. We may push ourselves to the limit, ignoring the signs of fatigue and stress. Yoga Nidra provides an opportunity to rest and rejuvenate the physical body.

The deep relaxation techniques used in the practice can help to release tension, reduce muscle stiffness, and improve circulation.

Yoga Nidra can also have a profound impact on our nervous system, helping to balance the sympathetic and parasympathetic branches.

This can lead to a decrease in the production of stress hormones such as cortisol and adrenaline, and an increase in the production of feel-good hormones such as endorphins and serotonin.

The practice can also help to regulate heart rate, blood pressure, and digestion, promoting overall health and well- being.

Healing the Spirit

Our spiritual well-being is often overlooked in our modern society. We may feel disconnected from ourselves,
others, and the world around us. Yoga Nidra can help to reawaken our spiritual essence and connect us to a deeper sense of purpose and meaning.

The practice can help us to tap into our inner wisdom, intuition, and creativity.

Yoga Nidra can also facilitate spiritual growth and transformation. By entering a state of deep relaxation, we can access the subconscious mind and explore the deeper layers of our consciousness.

This can lead to profound insights, healing, and spiritual

awakening. The practice can help us to let go of limiting beliefs and attachments, and open our hearts to love, compassion, and forgiveness.

Incorporating Yoga Nidra into Your Routine

If you're interested in experiencing the healing benefits of Yoga Nidra, there are several ways to incorporate the practice into your daily routine.

You can attend a Yoga Nidra class at a local studio or wellness center, or participate in a guided meditation online or through a mobile app. You can also practice Yoga Nidra on your own by following a recorded audio or video session.

To get the most out of your Yoga Nidra practice, it's important to create a quiet and comfortable space where you won't be disturbed. You can lie down on a yoga mat or bed, cover yourself with a blanket, and close your eyes.

Take a few deep breaths to relax your body and mind, and then follow the instructions of the facilitator as they guide you through the practice.

It's recommended to practice Yoga Nidra regularly to experience the full benefits of the practice. You can start with a short session of 15-20 minutes and gradually increase the duration as you become more comfortable with the practice.

Consistency is key to reaping the rewards of Yoga Nidra, so try to make it a regular part of your self-care routine.

In conclusion, Yoga Nidra is a powerful tool for healing the mind, body, and spirit. The practice offers a way to relax, recharge, and rejuvenate, allowing us to release stress, tension, and negative emotions.

 By incorporating Yoga Nidra into our daily routine, we can experience profound physical, mental, and spiritual benefits.

A Journey to Inner Peace

Nidra Yoga, also referred to as Yoga Nidra or Yogic Sleep, stands as a potent and transformative discipline guiding individuals towards inner tranquility and profound relaxation.

In the hustle and bustle of today's world, where stress and anxiety pervade daily life, Nidra Yoga emerges as a sanctuary, offering solace and connection with one's authentic essence.

At its core, Nidra Yoga encompasses guided meditation and relaxation techniques, facilitating entry into a realm of conscious deep sleep.

Unlike conventional meditation practices necessitating focused attention on a singular point or object, Nidra Yoga invites practitioners to relinquish effort and embrace the present moment fully.

Central to Nidra Yoga is the utilization of a guided script, orchestrating a journey through visualizations, body scans, and breathwork.

This script serves to alleviate bodily tension, pacify the mind, and dissolve emotional barriers. As individuals adhere to the guidance provided, they transition into a state of profound relaxation akin to sleep, yet retaining complete awareness and consciousness.

Typically practiced in a supine position, with closed eyes and full body support, Nidra Yoga facilitates total relaxation of body and mind.

This setup allows practitioners to release both physical and mental tension, fostering an environment conducive to inner peace and renewal. Sessions typically span 30-45 minutes, although duration may vary based on individual preferences and needs.

Engaging in regular Nidra Yoga practice offers a spectrum of benefits, both physical and mental. Among the advantages are:

- Reduced stress and anxiety: Nidra Yoga soothes the nervous system, alleviating stress and tension from the body. By immersing oneself in deep relaxation, worries and fears can dissipate, fostering a serene and tranquil state.

- Improved sleep: Nidra Yoga enhances sleep quality by inducing relaxation and combating insomnia. Practicing Nidra Yoga before bedtime prepares the body and mind for a peaceful night's rest.

- Increased focus and concentration: Nidra Yoga refines focus and concentration skills by pacifying the mind and minimizing distractions. Regular practice cultivates mental clarity and enhances productivity.

- Enhanced creativity and intuition: Nidra Yoga unlocks creativity and intuition by calming the mind and accessing inner wisdom. By connecting with one's true self through Nidra Yoga, individuals can unleash creative potential and make decisions grounded in clarity and insight.

- Emotional healing and release: Nidra Yoga liberates stored emotions and trauma from the body, facilitating the release of past hurts and wounds. Through Nidra Yoga practice, space for healing and transformation is created, fostering inner peace and wholeness.

In addition to these benefits, Nidra Yoga contributes to overall health and well-being by reducing inflammation, bolstering the immune system, and promoting relaxation. Integrating Nidra Yoga into daily routines fosters balance, harmony, and a deeper connection with oneself and the surrounding world.

Embarking on your Nidra Yoga journey is accessible and rewarding. You can begin by exploring guided scripts and recordings online or joining a class at a nearby yoga studio. Setting up a serene and undisturbed space for your practice is essential, where props like blankets, pillows, and eye masks can enhance your comfort and relaxation.

Approach Nidra Yoga with an open mind and a spirit of curiosity. Release any preconceived notions and judgments, immersing yourself fully in the present moment. Trust in the process of Nidra Yoga, allowing yourself to surrender to the experience, knowing it leads to inner peace and self-discovery.

In essence, Nidra Yoga offers a transformative journey towards inner peace and profound relaxation. Through regular practice, benefits such as decreased stress and anxiety, improved sleep, heightened focus and creativity, and emotional healing can be experienced.

Whether you're new to yoga or a seasoned practitioner, Nidra Yoga provides a path to reconnect with your authentic self and nurture a sense of peace and well-being. Take a deep breath, unwind, and embark on your Nidra Yoga journey today.

Chapter 5: The Art of Letting Go with Nidra Meditation

Letting go is a concept that is often easier said than done. We hold on to things, people, and emotions that no longer serve us, causing unnecessary stress and anxiety in our lives.

However, learning the art of letting go can be incredibly liberating and empowering. One powerful tool that can help in this process is Nidra Meditation.

Nidra Meditation, also known as Yoga Nidra or Yogic Sleep, is a guided meditation practice that induces a state of deep relaxation and conscious awareness.

It involves lying down in a comfortable position and following the instructions of a teacher or guide as they lead you through a series of relaxation techniques and visualizations.

The practice of Nidra Meditation can help you release physical, mental, and emotional tension, allowing you to experience a sense of deep peace and inner calm. It can also help you let go of negative thought patterns, limiting beliefs, and past traumas that may be holding you back from living your fullest life.

One of the key principles of Nidra Meditation is the concept of surrender. By surrendering to the present moment and letting go of the need to control or manipulate outcomes, you can cultivate a sense of trust and acceptance in yourself and the world around you. This practice of surrender can be incredibly transformative, helping you release attachments and expectations that no longer serve you.

Letting go with Nidra Meditation involves cultivating a sense of mindfulness and awareness of your thoughts, emotions, and sensations without judgment or attachment.

By observing these experiences with curiosity and compassion, you can begin to unravel the layers of conditioning and programming that may be keeping you stuck in patterns of suffering and resistance.

As you practice Nidra Meditation regularly, you may begin to notice a shift in your relationship to yourself and the world around you. You may start to feel more at ease with uncertainty and change, more compassionate towards yourself and others, and more connected to the present moment.

The art of letting go with Nidra Meditation is a journey of self-discovery and self-compassion. It requires patience, practice, and a willingness to explore the depths of your inner landscape with openness and curiosity.

 As you deepen your practice, you may find that you are able to release old wounds and traumas, forgive yourself and others, and embrace the beauty and impermanence of life.

Here are some tips for incorporating the art of letting go with

Nidra Meditation into your daily life:

1. Set aside time each day for a Nidra Meditation practice. Find a quiet, comfortable space where you can lie down and relax without distractions. You can use a guided meditation recording or practice on your own by focusing on your breath and body sensations.

2. Begin your practice by setting an intention to let go of anything that is no longer serving you. This could be a specific thought, emotion, belief, or habit that you are ready to release. Allow yourself to surrender to the present moment and trust in the process of transformation.

3. Notice any resistance or discomfort that arises during your practice. Instead of trying to push these feelings away, allow yourself to sit with them and explore where they may be coming from.

4. Practice self-compassion and forgiveness. As you let go of old wounds and traumas, be gentle with yourself and offer yourself the same love and understanding that you would give to a dear friend. Remember that healing is a process, and it is okay to take your time and go at your own pace.

5. Cultivate a sense of gratitude and appreciation for the present moment. By focusing on the blessings and beauty that surround you, you can shift your perspective from one of lack and scarcity to one of abundance and joy. Letting go with Nidra Meditation can help you see the world with fresh eyes and an

open heart.

6. Practice letting go in your daily life. As you go about your day, notice any attachments or expectations that arise and practice releasing them with mindfulness and awareness. By letting go of the need to control outcomes and surrendering to the flow of life, you can experience a greater sense of freedom and peace.

In conclusion, the art of letting go with Nidra Meditation is a powerful practice that can help you release old patterns, beliefs, and emotions that may be holding you back from living your fullest life.

By surrendering to the present moment, cultivating mindfulness and self-compassion, and embracing the process of transformation, you can experience a profound sense of liberation and inner peace.

Letting go with Nidra Meditation is not always easy, but with practice and patience, you can learn to release what no longer serves you and embrace the beauty and impermanence of life.

A Gateway to Emotional Healing

Nidra Yoga, often referred to as Yoga Nidra or Yogic Sleep, serves as a potent conduit for emotional healing. Rooted in ancient traditions, this guided meditation practice induces a profound state of relaxation, enabling practitioners to confront and release emotional barriers and past traumas that impede personal growth.

Described as a form of "psychic sleep," Nidra Yoga delves into the subconscious realm, facilitating the exploration and resolution of deep-seated emotional turmoil.

By immersing oneself in deep relaxation, individuals gain access to the recesses of their consciousness, allowing for the cathartic release of pent-up emotions and traumas that underpin conditions like stress, anxiety, and depression.

A fundamental advantage of Nidra Yoga lies in its gentle and non-invasive approach to emotional healing. Unlike conventional talk therapy, which may involve reliving traumatic experiences or engaging in challenging dialogues, Nidra Yoga offers a safe space for emotional release without re-traumatization.

This accessibility makes it particularly impactful for individuals hesitant to confront their emotions through traditional therapeutic methods.

Beyond its emotional healing capabilities, Nidra Yoga yields a myriad of physical and mental benefits. Scientifically validated, the practice alleviates stress, anxiety, and depression while enhancing sleep quality, nurturing creativity and intuition, and fostering overall well-being.

Through consistent engagement with Nidra Yoga, practitioners cultivate a profound sense of inner peace, mental clarity, and emotional equilibrium.

Nidra Yoga stands out for its effectiveness in emotional healing due to its multifaceted approach that addresses both the mind and body.

Integrating mindfulness, visualization, body awareness, and breathwork, this practice offers a comprehensive healing journey that delves into the core of emotional challenges.

By engaging with these aspects, Nidra Yoga facilitates the release of deep-seated emotional blockages and traumas, fostering profound healing and personal transformation.

Central to Nidra Yoga is the cultivation of self-compassion and self-care. Encouraging practitioners to embrace kindness and acceptance towards themselves, it becomes a nurturing sanctuary, especially for those grappling with self-criticism or low self-esteem.

Through the practice of self-compassion and self-care within Nidra Yoga, individuals learn to treat themselves with gentleness and empathy, leading to enhanced emotional well-being and self-acceptance.

Moreover, Nidra Yoga offers unparalleled accessibility, making it inclusive for individuals of all ages and fitness levels. Unlike certain yoga disciplines that demand physical prowess, Nidra Yoga merely requires practitioners to lie down and follow the guidance of a teacher or recording. This inclusivity renders it an ideal choice for beginners or those with physical constraints that may hinder other yoga practices.

Beyond accessibility, Nidra Yoga boasts remarkable adaptability, allowing for personalized sessions tailored to individual needs.

Whether addressing anxiety, depression, trauma, grief, or other emotional challenges, Nidra Yoga provides a safe and supportive environment for healing and growth.

Teachers and practitioners can tailor sessions to target specific emotional issues or goals, making it a versatile tool for emotional well-being and transformation.

In essence, Nidra Yoga serves as a potent avenue towards emotional healing. Through deep relaxation and subconscious exploration, practitioners can liberate themselves from emotional obstacles and past traumas.

Embracing principles of self-compassion, self-care, and holistic wellness, Nidra Yoga unfolds as a gentle yet powerful journey towards emotional equilibrium and inner tranquility.

Whether seeking release from emotional burdens, alleviation of stress and anxiety, or simply enhancing overall well-being,

Nidra Yoga stands as a valuable ally for emotional healing and individual evolution.

Nidra Meditation for Deep Relaxation

Nidra meditation, also referred to as Yoga Nidra, stands as a potent method for profound relaxation and restoration. This guided meditation technique facilitates a state of deep relaxation while maintaining conscious awareness.

Widely recognized for its capacity to alleviate stress, enhance sleep, and foster overall well-being, Nidra meditation emerges as a valuable tool for inner balance.

Engaging in Nidra meditation involves reclining in a comfortable posture, gently closing the eyes, and following the guidance of an experienced facilitator.

Through a sequence of relaxation practices like controlled breathing, systematic body scans, and guided imagery, participants journey into profound relaxation. As relaxation deepens, they may reach a state akin to sleep, yet marked by heightened awareness.

A notable advantage of Nidra meditation lies in its capacity to induce a level of relaxation often challenging to achieve through other modalities.

This profound state of relaxation holds potential to alleviate stress, diminish anxiety, and release tension from both body and mind. Moreover, it serves as a catalyst for enhancing sleep quality, fostering creativity, and nurturing overall well-being.

Nidra meditation offers particular benefits for individuals grappling with sleep disturbances like insomnia. By guiding practitioners into deep relaxation, Nidra meditation aids in pacifying the mind and body, facilitating easier sleep initiation and sustained restfulness throughout the night.

Many who incorporate Nidra meditation into their routine report experiencing more replenishing and revitalizing sleep cycles.

Beyond its tangible physical and mental advantages, Nidra meditation possesses profound spiritual dimensions. Through immersion in deep relaxation and heightened awareness, practitioners may access deeper realms of consciousness and establish a connection with their inner essence. This journey often culminates in heightened self-awareness, clarity of mind, and inner serenity.

To embark on a Nidra meditation session geared towards profound relaxation, seek out a serene and comfortable space to recline. Close your eyes and initiate the process by taking several deep breaths to center yourself.

Gradually release tension from each part of your body, commencing from your toes and ascending to your head. Allow any lingering stress or strain to dissipate as you focus on the rhythm of your breath and the sensations within your body.

With each passing moment, sink deeper into a state of tranquility and calmness. Surrender to the enveloping sense of relaxation and relinquish any stray thoughts or concerns that may surface. Place your trust in the process, allowing the guided instructions to lead you on this journey.

Through continued practice of Nidra meditation, you may observe a spectrum of benefits, encompassing both physical and mental realms.

These may include alleviated stress and anxiety, enhanced sleep quality, augmented concentration, and an overarching sense of well-being.

With consistent dedication, Nidra meditation can evolve into a potent instrument for profound relaxation and revitalization.

In summary, Nidra meditation stands as a potent avenue for delving into deep relaxation and rejuvenation. By ushering practitioners into a state of profound relaxation while maintaining conscious awareness, Nidra meditation holds the potential to alleviate stress, enhance sleep, and foster overall well-being.

Whether seeking relief from stress, enhancement of sleep quality, or a deeper connection with one's inner self, integrating Nidra meditation into daily practice can prove invaluable.

Chapter 6: Nidra Yoga: A Tool for Self-Transformation

Nidra Yoga, also referred to as Yoga Nidra or Yogic Sleep, serves as a potent catalyst for self-evolution and individual development. Rooted in ancient wisdom, this practice melds meditation, relaxation, and mindfulness to facilitate profound states of relaxation and self-awareness.

Through Nidra Yoga, practitioners delve into their inner reservoirs, shedding stress and tension, and nurturing a profound sense of inner peace and harmony.

In the realm of Nidra Yoga, participants recline in a comfortable posture, guided by a skilled instructor through a series of meditative steps. These steps encompass body scans, breath awareness exercises, and visualization techniques, each aimed at fostering relaxation and releasing tension.

The overarching objective of Nidra Yoga is to achieve a state of deep relaxation while retaining conscious awareness of one's thoughts, emotions, and bodily sensations.

At the core of Nidra Yoga lies its capacity to unlock the subconscious mind and access inner wisdom. By immersing in profound relaxation, practitioners transcend the mental chatter of the conscious mind, forging a connection with their authentic selves. This journey often unveils profound insights, triggers healing, and ignites transformative growth at a profound level.

Furthermore, Nidra Yoga emerges as a formidable ally in the pursuit of stress reduction and relaxation. In the hustle and bustle of contemporary life, individuals contend with a relentless barrage of stressors that can exact a toll on their holistic well-being. Nidra Yoga emerges as a sanctuary, offering a sanctuary for releasing stress, fostering relaxation, and reinstating equilibrium to the body and mind.

Nidra Yoga holds yet another advantage in its capacity to enhance sleep quality and induce restful slumber. For many grappling with insomnia or disrupted sleep patterns, the repercussions extend beyond mere tiredness, impacting their holistic well-being.

 By integrating regular Nidra Yoga practice, individuals can unwind both body and mind, shedding tension and fostering a serene inner state conducive to deep, restorative sleep.

Moreover, Nidra Yoga emerges as a potent catalyst for personal evolution and inner transformation. Within the folds of Nidra Yoga, practitioners embark on a journey through their inner realms, confronting fears and insecurities while nurturing self-acceptance and self-love.

 This odyssey cultivates heightened self-awareness, bolstered self-assurance, and a profound alignment with one's authentic essence.

Beyond its physical, mental, and emotional merits, Nidra Yoga also bestows spiritual rewards. By immersing in deep relaxation and reconnecting with their inner selves, individuals unlock a sense of unity with the cosmos and a profound resonance with their higher consciousness. This transcendent experience ushers in waves of peace, joy, and fulfillment that extend beyond the confines of the material realm.

In essence, Nidra Yoga stands as a potent instrument for self-evolution and individual development. Through consistent practice, participants can liberate themselves from stress and tension, elevate sleep quality, foster relaxation, and nurture a profound sense of inner tranquility and wellness.

 Regardless of whether you're a novice to yoga or a seasoned practitioner, Nidra Yoga presents a distinctive and transformative journey, empowering you to access your inner reservoirs and unleash your inherent capabilities.

For those intrigued by delving deeper into Nidra Yoga, exploring local classes or workshops can be an enriching avenue. Many yoga studios and wellness hubs host Nidra Yoga sessions led by seasoned instructors adept at guiding participants through the practice, enabling them to experience its benefits firsthand.

Alternatively, a wealth of guided Nidra Yoga meditations awaits online or through mobile apps, offering the convenience of practicing within the sanctuary of your own space.

In sum, Nidra Yoga emerges as a potent vehicle for self-transformation and personal growth. Its regular practice facilitates the shedding of stress, enhancement of sleep quality, promotion of relaxation, and nurturing of inner peace and well-being.

Whether your goal is stress reduction, sleep improvement, or inner connection, Nidra Yoga offers a distinctive and transformative journey, empowering you to unlock your true potential and lead a more enriching life.

Nidra Meditation for Sleep and Insomnia

Nidra meditation, also referred to as yoga nidra or yogic sleep, stands as a potent practice renowned for its efficacy in enhancing sleep quality and alleviating insomnia.

Rooted in ancient traditions, this technique employs deep relaxation and guided imagery to usher the practitioner into a state of consciousness that hovers between wakefulness and slumber.

 Through quieting the mind and unwinding tension within the body, nidra meditation facilitates restful sleep and fosters a holistic sense of well-being.

Insomnia, a pervasive sleep disorder affecting millions globally, stems from various factors such as stress, anxiety, depression, and irregular sleep patterns.

Amidst a plethora of treatment options, nidra meditation emerges as a natural and impactful approach to augment sleep quality and duration.

Nidra meditation operates by stimulating the parasympathetic nervous system, renowned for inducing relaxation and tranquility. Through the practice of profound relaxation techniques and immersion in soothing imagery, practitioners effectively mitigate stress and anxiety levels, paving the way for the body to embrace a state of profound relaxation conducive to sleep.

A fundamental advantage of nidra meditation lies in its capacity to quiet the mind and foster serenity. By anchoring attention to the present moment and relinquishing worries and distractions, individuals craft a tranquil mental space conducive to sleep initiation. This proves especially beneficial for those grappling with racing thoughts or bedtime anxiety.

Moreover, nidra meditation offers the additional benefit of releasing bodily tension. Many individuals accumulate physical stress and strain throughout the day, hindering relaxation and impeding sleep onset. Through consistent nidra meditation practice, practitioners liberate this tension, fostering a sense of bodily ease that facilitates seamless transition into sleep.

Another noteworthy advantage of nidra meditation in addressing sleep issues, particularly insomnia, is its capacity to enhance overall sleep quality.

By fostering deep relaxation and diminishing stress levels, this practice empowers individuals to attain more restful and revitalizing sleep experiences.

Consequently, this improvement in sleep quality often translates into heightened energy levels, uplifted mood, and enhanced overall health and well-being.

To engage in nidra meditation for sleep enhancement and insomnia alleviation, locate a serene and comfortable space to recline. With eyes closed, embark on a sequence of deep breaths to ease tension within the body and mind. Subsequently, immerse yourself in a guided meditation or visualization aimed at inducing relaxation and tranquility. This may involve directing attention to various body regions, envisioning serene settings, or repeating soothing affirmations.

Continued engagement with nidra meditation frequently yields observable enhancements in sleep patterns and overall wellness. Through consistent practice, individuals can cultivate the capacity to unwind both mentally and physically, facilitating swifter sleep onset and deeper sleep cycles.

Consequently, this fosters a more rejuvenating and revitalizing nocturnal rest, alongside bolstered mood and vitality throughout the day.

In conjunction with nidra meditation, integrating additional sleep-promoting strategies can further optimize sleep quality and mitigate insomnia.

These strategies encompass establishing a consistent sleep schedule, crafting a relaxing bedtime ritual, refraining from caffeine and screen exposure before sleep, and curating a conducive sleep environment.

By amalgamating these complementary approaches with nidra meditation, individuals can devise a comprehensive and holistic framework for enhancing sleep and fortifying overall well-being.

In essence, nidra meditation emerges as a potent practice for ameliorating sleep issues and assuaging insomnia concerns. By instilling deep relaxation, attenuating stress levels, and augmenting sleep quality, this time-honored method offers a natural and efficacious pathway to achieving restorative sleep.

Whether grappling with insomnia or striving to optimize sleep quality, nidra meditation stands poised as a valuable asset within one's sleep hygiene regimen.

Connecting Mind, Body, and Spirit

Nidra Yoga, known as Yoga Nidra or Yogic Sleep, stands as a profound and transformative practice, inviting practitioners into a holistic connection with their mind, body, and spirit.

Rooted in ancient yogic and meditative teachings, this practice aims to facilitate deep relaxation, inner peace, and spiritual awakening.

Derived from Sanskrit, "Nidra" denotes sleep, yet within Nidra Yoga, it connotes a state of conscious relaxation attained through guided meditation.

Unlike conventional meditation forms that emphasize alertness, Nidra Yoga encourages participants to embrace profound relaxation, enabling access to the subconscious realm and fostering connection with inner thoughts, emotions, and sensations.

Typically performed in a reclined position, practitioners of Nidra Yoga lie comfortably, eyes shut, supported by props like blankets and pillows. Commencing with guided relaxation techniques, the practice eases the mind and releases bodily tension.

As practitioners delve into deep relaxation, they embark on a journey guided by visualizations, affirmations, and body scans, deepening their self-awareness and internal connection.

Central to Nidra Yoga is the principle of interconnectedness between body and mind. By relaxing the body, practitioners concurrently calm the mind, accessing inner tranquility.

Through this practice, individuals liberate themselves from physical and mental tensions, alleviating stress, anxiety, and enhancing overall well-being.

Beyond its physical and mental merits, Nidra Yoga serves as a catalyst for spiritual growth and self-discovery. By delving into inner thoughts and emotions, practitioners unearth insights into their authentic selves, fostering profound self-awareness and self-acceptance.

 Thus, Nidra Yoga transcends mere relaxation, evolving into a transformative journey of holistic connection and spiritual exploration.

Nidra Yoga embodies a journey of surrender and release, urging practitioners to detach from thoughts, emotions, and desires, embracing the present moment fully.

Through this surrender, individuals connect with their higher selves, transcending ego constraints to uncover inner peace and contentment.

A cornerstone of Nidra Yoga lies in its capacity to access the subconscious mind, delving into inner wisdom and intuition. Guided visualizations and affirmations pave the path for practitioners to explore deeper consciousness layers, revealing profound truths about themselves and their existence.

Moreover, Nidra Yoga serves as a conduit for self-healing, offering a space to shed emotional wounds, traumas, and detrimental patterns hindering one's growth.

By delving into their innermost selves and releasing these barriers, individuals embrace liberation and empowerment, stepping into a life of authenticity and fulfillment.

Beyond spiritual and emotional realms, Nidra Yoga extends tangible physical benefits. By immersing in deep relaxation, practitioners alleviate muscle tension, reduce blood pressure, enhance circulation, and fortify the immune system.

This holistic approach fosters vitality, energy, and overall well-being, nurturing a harmonious balance within body, mind, and spirit.
Nidra Yoga stands as a holistic pathway to holistic well-being, harmonizing the mind, body, and spirit in a profoundly transformative manner.

Whether seeking stress relief, mental clarity enhancement, or spiritual deepening, Nidra Yoga presents an accessible and potent avenue for self-discovery and inner tranquility.

In essence, Nidra Yoga beckons us to commune with our inner essence, delving into realms of peace, clarity, and completeness that transcend egoic confines.

Through embracing deep relaxation and surrender, we unlock inner wisdom, untangle emotional knots, and commune with our higher selves. Nidra Yoga fosters a state of equilibrium and resonance, enabling us to embrace life with authenticity and richness.

Irrespective of yoga proficiency, Nidra Yoga extends a potent and transformative practice, facilitating profound connections with the mind, body, and spirit. It serves as a guiding light on the journey toward inner harmony and holistic wellness

Chapter 7: The Science behind Nidra Meditation

Nidra meditation, also known as yoga nidra or yogic sleep, stands as a potent fusion of profound relaxation and mindfulness techniques. It involves reclining in a comfortable position, enabling both body and mind to sink into deep relaxation while maintaining heightened awareness.

This practice has surged in popularity due to its remarkable capacity to alleviate stress, enhance sleep quality, and elevate overall well-being.

At the core of nidra meditation lies its scientific foundation, rooted in its ability to activate the parasympathetic nervous system—the body's natural relaxation mechanism.

In times of stress or anxiety, the sympathetic nervous system takes charge, triggering increased heart rate, shallow breathing, and heightened vigilance.

Nidra meditation acts as a counterbalance, stimulating the parasympathetic nervous system to induce relaxation, slow the heart rate, and facilitate profound rejuvenation.

Central to nidra meditation is the technique of body scanning, wherein practitioners systematically direct attention to various body parts, beginning from the toes and ascending to the head. This meticulous process aids in releasing stored tension and stress, fostering physical relaxation and a profound sense of serenity. By anchoring awareness in bodily sensations, the mind relinquishes its hold on racing thoughts, ushering in a state of tranquil repose.

Moreover, nidra meditation harnesses visualizations and affirmations to nurture positive emotions and beliefs. Throughout a session, practitioners may immerse themselves in serene imagery—be it a tranquil beach or a lush forest—or repeat affirmations such as "I am calm and at peace."

These mental constructs serve to reprogram the subconscious mind, displacing negative thought patterns with affirming ones, fostering inner harmony, and cultivating a profound sense of well-being and tranquility.

Studies have highlighted the myriad benefits of nidra meditation for both physical and mental health. Evidence suggests that regular nidra practice can effectively alleviate stress, anxiety, and depression while fostering improved sleep quality and overall well-being.

For instance, research published in the Journal of Alternative and Complementary Medicine showcased significant reductions in stress and anxiety levels among nidra meditation practitioners compared to a control group.

Moreover, nidra meditation extends its positive influence to physical health, with studies indicating reductions in blood pressure, inflammation, and enhanced immune function. A study in the International Journal of Yoga Therapy observed lower cortisol levels and increased melatonin levels—markers of deep relaxation and rejuvenating sleep—among nidra meditation participants.

Furthermore, the cognitive benefits of nidra meditation are noteworthy. Regular practice has been associated with enhanced attention, memory, and cognitive flexibility.

Research published in Frontiers in Human Neuroscience revealed improvements in cognitive function and decreased mind-wandering among nidra meditation practitioners, indicating heightened focus and concentration.

In essence, the science behind nidra meditation underscores its profound impact on both body and mind. By activating the parasympathetic nervous system, fostering physical relaxation, and boosting cognitive function, nidra meditation offers a holistic approach to stress reduction, improved sleep, and enhanced overall well-being.

Regardless of whether you're just starting your meditation journey or have been practicing for a while, integrating nidra meditation into your daily routine can be instrumental in fostering a profound sense of inner peace and equilibrium in your life.

A Path to Spiritual Awakening

Nidra Yoga, also recognized as Yoga Nidra or Yogic Sleep, stands as a potent pathway toward profound spiritual enlightenment.

This ancient yogic practice, rooted in teachings from esteemed Indian scriptures like the Upanishads and the Bhagavad Gita, has served as a means for seekers to attain spiritual awakening and liberation over millennia.

"Nidra" in Sanskrit translates to sleep, symbolizing a state of conscious deep relaxation where practitioners hover between wakefulness and slumber.

Engaging in Nidra Yoga involves reclining in a comfortable position and surrendering to the guidance of a seasoned instructor or facilitator.

Through a series of meticulously crafted instructions, participants embark on a journey of body scans, breath awareness, visualizations, and affirmations, all aimed at inducing profound relaxation and inner attunement.

As practitioners delve deeper into relaxation, they may encounter sensations of weightlessness and heightened awareness of their inner landscape—thoughts, emotions, and bodily sensations.

Central to Nidra Yoga's allure is its capacity to alleviate stress, tension, and anxiety entrenched within the body and mind. By delving into profound relaxation, individuals shed layers of physical and mental strain, paving the way for tranquility and serenity to blossom.

 This transformative release holds profound implications for overall well-being, given the detrimental impact chronic stress and tension can have on health, contributing to conditions like heart disease, hypertension, and depression.

Beyond its physical advantages, Nidra Yoga serves as a potent catalyst for spiritual evolution and self-discovery. Through the gateway of deep relaxation, practitioners delve into their subconscious minds, unraveling entrenched beliefs, fears, and patterns that hinder their full potential.

This journey of self-inquiry fosters profound introspection, granting individuals a deeper comprehension of their essence and paving the path to inner peace and fulfillment.

Moreover, Nidra Yoga empowers individuals to harness their intuition and creativity. By quieting the mind and delving into the subconscious realm, practitioners tap into a wellspring of inner wisdom and inspiration, birthing novel insights and unleashing untapped creative reservoirs.

 For artisans, writers, and creative souls, this process proves invaluable in surmounting creative barriers and unlocking boundless creative expression.

A distinguishing facet of Nidra Yoga lies in its capacity to induce a state of profound relaxation akin to hours of restorative sleep. Particularly beneficial for those grappling with insomnia or sleep disturbances, Nidra Yoga fosters deep, rejuvenating sleep, amplifying overall sleep quality. Remarkably, many enthusiasts attest to feeling more revitalized and invigorated following a Nidra Yoga session than after a full night's slumber.

Furthermore, Nidra Yoga facilitates access to altered states of consciousness and spiritual realms. By surrendering to deep relaxation, practitioners open conduits to higher planes of awareness, forging connections with spiritual guides, ancestral energies, and their higher selves.

These transcendent encounters yield profound revelations and spiritual awakenings, igniting transformative shifts in individuals' lives.

In essence, Nidra Yoga stands as a profound practice catalyzing spiritual enlightenment and metamorphosis.

Through immersing themselves in profound relaxation and inner awareness, practitioners of Nidra Yoga can liberate themselves from the grip of stress, tension, and anxiety that plagues both body and mind.

This practice unveils deeply ingrained beliefs and patterns, while fostering a connection with intuition and creativity. Moreover, it serves as a gateway to accessing altered states of consciousness and spiritual realms.

Whether one is a novice or seasoned practitioner, Nidra Yoga presents an unparalleled journey towards spiritual evolution, self-discovery, and inner serenity.

Nidra Meditation for Anxiety
and Depression

Yoga Nidra, also called nidra meditation or yogic sleep, stands as a potent practice renowned for alleviating symptoms associated with anxiety and depression. Rooted in ancient yogic traditions, this profound relaxation technique has served as a cornerstone for physical, mental, and emotional healing across centuries.

In contemporary society, anxiety and depression loom as prevalent mental health challenges, impacting countless individuals regardless of age. While conventional treatments like medication and therapy hold merit, an increasing number of people are seeking solace in alternative modalities such as meditation to address their symptoms and foster holistic well-being.

Nidra meditation unfolds as a guided practice typically conducted in a reclined position conducive to comfort. Through a series of verbal cues, practitioners are led into a state of profound relaxation, facilitating access to the subconscious realm and the release of accumulated tension and stress within the body.

A pivotal aspect of nidra meditation's efficacy in mitigating anxiety and depression lies in its activation of the parasympathetic nervous system, often referred to as the "rest and digest" system. In states of chronic stress or anxiety, the sympathetic nervous system, responsible for the "fight or flight" response, remains incessantly engaged, precipitating a spectrum of physical and mental health concerns.

By stimulating the parasympathetic nervous system via nidra meditation, individuals can counterbalance the detrimental effects of chronic stress, fostering a climate of relaxation and recuperation within the body. This serves to alleviate symptoms associated with anxiety and depression, including intrusive thoughts, feelings of overwhelm, and physical tension.

Engaging in Nidra meditation aids in quieting the mind and fostering a profound sense of inner peace and tranquility. Amidst the turmoil of anxiety or depression, our thoughts often spiral into negativity, inundating us with overwhelming emotions.

Through the practice of Nidra meditation, we learn to observe these thoughts impartially, fostering a sense of detachment from their grip.

This detachment cultivates a more positive and balanced outlook on our experiences, diminishing the influence of negative thought patterns on our mental well-being. By nurturing inner peace and calmness through Nidra meditation, we equip ourselves with greater resilience and clarity to navigate life's trials.

Beyond its mental health benefits, Nidra meditation extends its positive influence to our physical well-being. Prolonged stress and anxiety can exact a toll on the body, manifesting in conditions such as high blood pressure, digestive issues, and compromised immune function.

Regular practice of Nidra meditation serves to alleviate the physical manifestations of stress and anxiety, promoting holistic health and vitality. This revitalization empowers us to feel more energized, focused, and robust in confronting life's adversities.

For those grappling with anxiety or depression, integrating Nidra meditation into their daily routine can serve as a potent means of symptom management and healing. Here are some pointers to commence your journey with Nidra meditation:

1. Create a serene and cozy environment devoid of distractions where you can recline comfortably. Consider using a yoga mat or blanket for support and warmth.

1. Establish an intention for your practice. Whether it's easing anxiety, uplifting your mood, or simply unwinding, setting a specific goal can guide your nidra meditation session.

2. Utilize guided nidra meditation sessions. Numerous online resources offer guided audio recordings and videos to support and enhance your meditation experience, aiding in navigating the practice effectively.

3. Center yourself with your breath. Embrace the breath as your anchor to the present moment during nidra

meditation. Observe the rhythmic flow of your breath, allowing it to lead you into profound relaxation.

4. Cultivate self-compassion. Throughout your nidra meditation journey, extend kindness to yourself and accept any thoughts or emotions that arise without judgment. Recognize that healing is a gradual process, and you deserve love and compassion.

5. Ease back into awareness. When concluding your nidra meditation, gradually reconnect with your body and surroundings. Take a moment to stretch gently, allowing yourself a smooth transition back into your day.

By incorporating nidra meditation into your daily regimen, you can unlock its potent benefits for managing anxiety and depression. With consistent practice, you may notice improvements in symptoms, a brighter mood, and overall enhanced well-being.

Remember, nidra meditation serves as just one tool in your mental health arsenal. Seek guidance from qualified healthcare professionals if you're grappling with severe anxiety or depression. With dedication and commitment, nidra meditation can become a valuable ally in your journey toward healing and inner peace amidst life's trials.

Chapter 8: Embracing the Present Moment

Nidra Yoga, known as Yoga Nidra or Yogic Sleep, stands as a potent meditation practice enabling individuals to reach profound relaxation while retaining consciousness. Originating in ancient India, it has surged in popularity recently, hailed for its stress reduction, sleep enhancement, and mindfulness cultivation.

Central to Nidra Yoga is embracing the present moment, shedding the weight of past and future concerns. By anchoring in the present, practitioners unlock a serene tranquility that extends into their everyday existence, especially benefitting those grappling with anxiety, insomnia, and stress-related challenges.

Fundamental to Nidra Yoga is the art of surrendering to the experience. Rather than dictating or directing the meditation, participants are urged to relinquish control and allow the process to unfold organically.

While relinquishing control may pose a challenge, particularly for those accustomed to maintaining a tight grip, it serves as a prerequisite for accessing the profound relaxation Nidra Yoga offers.

Guided imagery and visualization form another cornerstone of Nidra Yoga. In a typical session, instructors lead participants through a sequence of visualizations aimed at inducing relaxation and releasing thoughts and concerns. Ranging from envisioning tranquil beaches to serene forests, these visualizations foster a deep sense of peace and calm.

Beyond relaxation and stress alleviation, Nidra Yoga yields tangible physical benefits. Plunging into deep relaxation, practitioners witness a decline in heart rate, a decrease in blood pressure, and an overall enhancement in well-being.

This holistic impact on mental and physical health renders Nidra Yoga a valuable asset for individuals seeking to elevate their quality of life.

Nidra Yoga's effectiveness stems from its capacity to access the subconscious mind, a realm often untapped in waking states. Through deep relaxation, practitioners unlock this reservoir of hidden beliefs and patterns, offering a pathway to address negative thought cycles and self-limiting beliefs.

By delving into this subconscious realm, individuals can rewrite their mental scripts, fostering more constructive and positive thought patterns.

Beyond its cognitive and physical benefits, Nidra Yoga extends spiritual advantages. Immersed in profound relaxation and attuned to the present, participants often feel a profound unity with the cosmos, tapping into their innate wisdom.

This heightened connection fosters a deeper sense of life's purpose and significance, amplifying their connection to the world and those around them.

In essence, Nidra Yoga stands as a potent practice encompassing myriad benefits for mind and body alike. By embracing the here and now and relinquishing attachment to past and future, practitioners bask in deep relaxation, alleviating stress, enhancing sleep, and nurturing mindfulness. Whether novice or seasoned, Nidra Yoga offers a transformative journey towards enhanced peace and well-being.

For those intrigued by Nidra Yoga, seeking guidance from a qualified instructor is paramount. Their expertise ensures proper execution and maximizes the benefits of the practice.

You have several options for engaging in Nidra Yoga. You can explore local classes or workshops online or try practicing at home with guided meditation recordings or videos.

When setting up for Nidra Yoga, creating a serene environment is key. Find a quiet space and consider dimming the lights, lighting a candle, or playing gentle music to foster tranquility. Enhance your comfort with props like blankets, pillows, or eye masks.

During your Nidra Yoga session, prioritize your breath and allow yourself to fully unwind. Acknowledge any thoughts or emotions that arise, letting them pass without judgment, and refocus on the present moment. Consistent practice with an open mind can unlock the manifold benefits of Nidra Yoga.

In essence, Nidra Yoga empowers you to embrace the now and release attachment to past and future. By delving into deep relaxation and connecting with your subconscious, you unlock mental, physical, and spiritual well-being. Whether seeking stress reduction, sleep improvement, or mindfulness cultivation, Nidra Yoga offers a pathway to greater peace and vitality in your life.

Nidra Meditation for Inner Peace and Calm

Nidra Meditation, also referred to as Yoga Nidra or Yogic Sleep, is a potent technique for fostering inner tranquility and serenity. Rooted in ancient wisdom, this practice combines deep relaxation with guided meditation to facilitate a state of consciousness that bridges wakefulness and sleep.

Through consistent engagement with Nidra Meditation, individuals can unlock profound relaxation, alleviate stress and anxiety, enhance sleep quality, and nurture a deep sense of inner peace and calm.

With origins spanning millennia across diverse spiritual traditions like Yoga and Buddhism, Nidra Meditation is a guided practice typically conducted while lying in a comfortable position.

Participants follow verbal instructions provided by a teacher or pre-recorded guide. The session typically commences with a body scan, guiding awareness through each part of the body to release tension and induce profound relaxation.

Subsequent stages involve guided visualizations and breath awareness, further soothing the mind and facilitating deep relaxation.

A primary advantage of Nidra Meditation lies in its capacity to mitigate stress and anxiety. During periods of stress, the body triggers a fight-or-flight response, releasing stress hormones like cortisol and adrenaline.

These physiological reactions can detrimentally impact both physical and mental well-being, manifesting as symptoms such as high blood pressure, insomnia, and depression. Through Nidra Meditation, individuals activate the body's relaxation response, counterbalancing the stress response and fostering a state of tranquility and equilibrium.

Moreover, Nidra Meditation holds promise for improving sleep quality. Many individuals grapple with insomnia or restless sleep, which detrimentally affects overall health and vitality.

By integrating Nidra Meditation into their bedtime routine, individuals can alleviate bodily and mental tension, facilitating ease in falling asleep and sustaining rest throughout the night.

The profound relaxation induced by Nidra Meditation also contributes to the enhancement of sleep quality, fostering a more rejuvenating and revitalizing restorative experience.

In our modern, bustling world, finding moments of peace and tranquility can be challenging. However, Nidra Meditation offers a sanctuary for cultivating inner calm amidst the chaos.

Beyond its renowned benefits of stress reduction and improved sleep, Nidra Meditation provides a sacred space to reconnect with oneself, quiet the restless mind, and bask in the serenity of the present moment.

Through regular practice, one can nurture a profound inner peace that permeates every aspect of life, empowering them to gracefully navigate life's inevitable trials.

To embark on a journey of inner peace and calm through Nidra Meditation, carve out a serene and undisturbed space where you can comfortably recline.

Close your eyes and initiate your practice by taking a series of deep, grounding breaths to anchor yourself and ease into relaxation.

Begin a systematic journey of awareness through your body, starting from your toes and ascending gently to the crown of your head. With each exhale, release any tension or discomfort you encounter along the way.

As the body settles into a state of tranquility, shift your focus to the rhythm of your breath. Observe its natural ebb and flow, serving as a steadfast anchor amidst the swirling currents of the mind.

Alternatively, immerse yourself in a guided visualization—a serene beach, a tranquil forest—to deepen relaxation and quiet mental chatter. Surrender to the profound stillness enveloping you, relinquishing any fleeting thoughts or worries that may arise.

Continuing your journey with Nidra Meditation, you may find a serene tranquility enveloping you. This profound peace arises from the deep relaxation and mindfulness fostered by the practice. As you release the whirlwind of thoughts and connect with your inner being, you can experience a tranquility that surpasses the trials and tribulations of daily life.

In addition to personal practice, attending guided Nidra Meditation sessions or workshops can enrich your experience. Many yoga studios and meditation centers offer these sessions, led by seasoned instructors who can deepen your understanding and immersion in the practice.

Through a blend of guided meditation, breath awareness, and relaxation techniques, these classes foster a profound state of inner peace and calm.

In essence, Nidra Meditation serves as a potent tool for nurturing inner peace and tranquility. Regular practice can alleviate stress and anxiety, enhance sleep quality, and instill a lasting sense of serenity throughout your day.

 Whether you embark on solo practice or engage in guided sessions with a teacher, the transformative benefits of Nidra Meditation await your exploration. Delve into this ancient practice and uncover the tranquil depths within you.

A Practice of Surrender and Release

Nidra Yoga, or Yoga Nidra, stands as a potent practice intertwining deep relaxation and meditation. Rooted in ancient yogic teachings, it offers a guided journey into profound relaxation while maintaining conscious awareness. This practice serves as a valuable tool for stress reduction, healing, and self-discovery, harnessing the wisdom of millennia-old traditions.

With origins traced back to the ancient Hindu texts, particularly the Upanishads, Nidra Yoga unveils pathways to self-realization and enlightenment.

Its essence lies in the practice of lying down in comfort and surrendering to the guidance of a teacher or recorded instructions.

Through a series of relaxation techniques, body scans, visualizations, and affirmations, practitioners embark on a journey to release tension, stress, and negative emotions from the body and mind.

Central to Nidra Yoga is the art of surrender. Here, practitioners are urged to relinquish control and immerse themselves in the present moment.

This act of surrender, though challenging amidst the backdrop of a control-driven society, fosters trust in the process of relaxation and healing. By releasing attachment to outcomes and expectations, practitioners embrace the flow of relaxation, paving the way for profound transformation.

Moreover, Nidra Yoga emphasizes the practice of release. Through its deep relaxation and meditative techniques, practitioners unravel layers of tension, stress, and negative emotions stored within. This liberation brings forth a sense of freedom and lightness, shedding the burdens that weigh upon the soul.

In essence, Nidra Yoga stands as a timeless practice, offering a sanctuary for seekers of peace, healing, and self-discovery. Its profound teachings, rooted in ancient wisdom, guide practitioners on a journey of surrender, release, and profound transformation.

The transformative potential of Nidra Yoga spans across various facets of well-being, offering a plethora of profound benefits. From stress reduction and improved sleep to heightened relaxation, enhanced creativity, and deepened self-awareness, the rewards of Nidra Yoga are both abundant and far-reaching.

Moreover, this practice holds therapeutic promise for individuals grappling with conditions like anxiety, depression, PTSD, and other mental health challenges.

One of the remarkable attributes of Nidra Yoga lies in its inclusivity. Regardless of age, fitness level, or prior experience with yoga, anyone can engage in this practice. Conveniently accessible from the comfort of one's own home, Nidra Yoga merely requires a tranquil space, a cozy mat or blanket, and either a guided meditation recording or a knowledgeable teacher to lead the way.

For those intrigued by the prospect of delving into Nidra Yoga, a multitude of resources await exploration. Whether it's accessing guided meditation recordings online, participating in Nidra Yoga classes at a nearby studio, or arranging private sessions with a seasoned instructor, avenues for initiation abound.

In essence, Nidra Yoga beckons as a pathway to surrender and release, offering profound relaxation, healing, and self-discovery. Through the act of relinquishing control and embracing the present moment, practitioners can liberate themselves from the grip of tension, stress, and negative emotions entrenched within body and mind.

As a result, a newfound sense of liberation, buoyancy, and tranquility unfolds, permeating every facet of life. So, why not embark on the journey of Nidra Yoga and witness firsthand the transformative potency of this ancient practice?

Chapter 9: Nidra Meditation for Healing and Renewal

Nidra meditation, also referred to as yoga nidra or yogic sleep, stands as a potent practice for rejuvenation and restoration. Rooted in ancient wisdom, this technique facilitates a profound state of relaxation while maintaining conscious awareness.

Through a guided journey of mental stages, nidra meditation holds the capacity to unravel tension, alleviate stress, and foster holistic well-being.

Engaging in nidra meditation involves reclining in a comfortable posture, gently closing the eyes, and heeding the guidance of a skilled facilitator or pre-recorded audio. As the practitioner traverses a sequence of body scans, breath awareness exercises, visualizations, and affirmations, the body eases into relaxation, and the mind finds serenity.

A hallmark benefit of nidra meditation lies in its activation of the parasympathetic nervous system, known as the "rest and digest" response. This counteracts the detrimental effects of chronic stress, fostering profound relaxation with far-reaching implications for physical and mental health.

Scientifically supported, nidra meditation showcases a spectrum of advantages, including anxiety reduction, enhanced sleep quality, mood elevation, and an overall sense of well-being.

Moreover, it serves as a potent tool for healing and renewal, tapping into the body's innate capacity for self-recovery.

Throughout the nidra meditation journey, practitioners may encounter a profound sense of tranquility, deep relaxation, and an acute presence in the moment. This heightened state of awareness facilitates the release of emotional and physical burdens, fosters self-healing, and nurtures inner peace and harmony.

Nidra meditation emerges as a particularly valuable resource for individuals grappling with chronic pain, insomnia, anxiety, depression, PTSD, or other stress-related conditions. By instilling relaxation and alleviating stress, nidra meditation holds the promise of symptom improvement and an enhanced quality of life.

Beyond its therapeutic advantages, nidra meditation serves as a conduit for revitalizing and invigorating the mind, body, and spirit. Through immersion in profound relaxation, practitioners shed old cognitive and behavioral patterns, relinquish negative emotions, and carve out room for fresh insights and viewpoints to blossom.

Nidra meditation is adaptable, fitting seamlessly into daily rituals or utilized on an as-needed basis to navigate stress, foster tranquility, and bolster the journey of healing and rejuvenation.

Whether practiced in the comfort of home, within the serene ambiance of a yoga studio, or integrated into a comprehensive treatment regimen in medical environments, its versatility renders it accessible to all seeking holistic well-being.

To embark on your journey with nidra meditation for healing and renewal, carve out a serene and cozy space where you can recline and unwind without disturbances. You might opt for a guided meditation session led by an experienced facilitator or utilize recorded instructions to steer you through the practice.

Initiate the process by taking several deep breaths to ground yourself and ease the tension in your body. With eyes gently closed, shift your focus to your breath, observing its natural ebb and flow. Surrender to the gravitational pull, allowing your body to melt into the supportive surface beneath you.

Gradually, direct your awareness to different regions of your body, commencing with your toes and ascending toward your head.

Acknowledge any pockets of tightness or discomfort, and with each exhalation, consciously release them. Permit every muscle group to soften and relinquish any residual resistance or strain.
As you delve deeper into relaxation, you may embark on visualization journeys or recite affirmations aimed at fostering healing and revitalization. Picture a luminous aura or a stream of rejuvenating energy coursing through your being, purifying and invigorating every cell and fiber.

Throughout this process, maintain an open-hearted receptivity to any sensations, emotions, or insights that surface. Embrace the unfolding journey of nidra meditation, trusting in its profound capacity for healing and renewal.

Once the meditation concludes, gradually reawaken your body and mind. Wiggle your fingers and toes, stretch your limbs, and gently reopen your eyes. Take a moment to assess how you feel post-practice, noting any shifts in your physical, mental, or emotional state.

Through consistent practice, nidra meditation can catalyze healing and renewal across all dimensions of your existence. Whether grappling with physical discomfort, emotional turbulence, or simply seeking deeper serenity and wellness, nidra meditation stands as a steadfast ally in your quest for health and wholeness.

In essence, nidra meditation emerges as a potent conduit for healing and rejuvenation, fostering stress reduction, relaxation, and holistic well-being. By delving into states of profound relaxation and conscious presence, practitioners unlock the body's innate capacity for self-repair and renewal.

Irrespective of whether you're a novice or seasoned meditator, nidra meditation holds promise as a pivotal element of your self-care regimen. Integrate this ancient practice into your daily routine to harness its transformative potential, and unveil a realm of deep relaxation and mindful awareness. Embrace the gift of nidra meditation and embark on a journey of profound renewal and inner transformation.

A Journey to Wholeness

Nidra Yoga, referred to as Yoga Nidra or Yogic Sleep, stands as a transformative practice guiding individuals towards inner harmony. Rooted in ancient wisdom, this yoga form serves as a guided meditation method, fostering profound relaxation and inner connection.

Within the realm of Nidra Yoga, practitioners traverse a state of consciousness bridging wakefulness and slumber, facilitating access to the subconscious to release tension, stress, and negativity.

Engaging in Nidra Yoga involves reclining in comfort, shutting the eyes, and adhering to the guidance of a seasoned instructor. Commencing with a meticulous body scan, practitioners direct attention to each bodily region, liberating any stored tension. Subsequent visualizations and affirmations cultivate mental serenity and inner tranquility.

A primary allure of Nidra Yoga lies in its capacity to induce deep relaxation and alleviate stress. Amidst today's frenetic pace, where relaxation is often overlooked, chronic stress and anxiety proliferate. Nidra Yoga serves as an antidote, ushering practitioners into a state of profound relaxation conducive to healing and renewal.

Furthermore, Nidra Yoga fosters an intimate connection with one's inner being. Through guided meditation and visualization, individuals delve into the subconscious realm, unveiling concealed emotions and aspirations. This journey of self-discovery empowers personal growth and facilitates positive life transformations.

Moreover, Nidra Yoga boasts prowess in enhancing sleep quality and fostering restorative rest. Amidst the prevalence of sleep disturbances and insomnia, Nidra Yoga offers solace. Regular practice instills relaxation techniques, enabling individuals to ease into slumber and maintain restful sleep cycles.

In essence, Nidra Yoga serves as a gateway to inner harmony and holistic well-being. With its profound relaxation and introspective elements, it nurtures the mind, body, and spirit. Embrace the transformative potential of Nidra Yoga to embark on a journey of self-discovery and renewal, fostering inner peace and vitality in the midst of life's tumultuous currents.

Beyond its physical and mental advantages, Nidra Yoga transcends into a spiritual realm, enabling practitioners to forge a connection with their higher selves and attain inner peace and unity. By quieting the mind and embracing the present moment, individuals delve into a profound sense of harmony with the cosmos and a profound communion with the divine.

Nidra Yoga encompasses a comprehensive approach to well-being, addressing the physical, mental, emotional, and spiritual facets of human existence.

Through guided meditation, visualization, and deep relaxation, practitioners undergo profound healing and metamorphosis across all dimensions. Whether seeking stress relief, enhanced sleep, self-discovery, or spiritual deepening, Nidra Yoga emerges as a potent instrument for fostering equilibrium and wholeness.

For those intrigued by the journey of Nidra Yoga, a myriad of resources await exploration. From classes and workshops at yoga studios, wellness centers, to retreats worldwide, opportunities abound to embark on this transformative expedition.

Additionally, the digital realm offers a wealth of online resources, including guided meditations, instructional videos, and insightful articles, facilitating a deeper understanding of Nidra Yoga and its life-enhancing potential.

In essence, Nidra Yoga beckons individuals on a path to completeness, offering an immersive and transcendent experience for practitioners of all levels.

Whether novices or seasoned yogis, Nidra Yoga promises relaxation, rejuvenation, and profound inner connection. By integrating this ancient practice into daily routines, the rewards of deep relaxation, stress alleviation, improved sleep, and spiritual evolution become attainable.

Embark on the transformative odyssey of Nidra Yoga today and unlock its boundless potential for holistic well-being and spiritual growth.

Nidra Meditation for Mental Clarity and Focus

Nidra meditation, known as yoga nidra or yogic sleep, stands as a potent tool for sharpening mental clarity and focus. This ancient practice intertwines deep relaxation and guided meditation to soothe the mind and body, ushering practitioners into a realm of profound awareness and inner tranquility.

Regular engagement with nidra meditation unveils the potential to elevate mental clarity, enrich focus, and foster a heightened sense of well-being.

For individuals grappling with stress, anxiety, or insomnia, nidra meditation offers a sanctuary of solace. By immersing oneself in deep relaxation through nidra meditation, the grip of tension loosens, and the mind finds serenity, paving the way for enhanced mental acuity and concentration.

Liberated from the shackles of worries and distractions, practitioners can immerse themselves more deeply in the present moment.

A cornerstone benefit of nidra meditation lies in its capacity to silence the cacophony of thoughts and reduce mental clutter. Through nidra meditation, one learns to witness thoughts without entanglement, fostering mental clarity and inner harmony. This newfound clarity empowers individuals to approach tasks with sharper focus and concentration, thereby amplifying productivity and performance.

Moreover, nidra meditation serves as a catalyst for honing the ability to remain present and anchored in the moment. By nurturing mindfulness during nidra meditation, practitioners train their minds to remain rooted in the present instant, relinquishing preoccupation with the past or future. This cultivated presence facilitates sustained focus on current endeavors, nurturing mental clarity and refining decision-making prowess.

Beyond sharpening mental clarity and focus, nidra meditation offers a holistic approach to improving overall well-being. By immersing oneself in deep relaxation during nidra meditation, the practice extends benefits such as stress reduction, anxiety alleviation, enhanced sleep quality, and mood elevation.

This amalgamation of effects fosters a profound sense of mental clarity and emotional equilibrium, empowering individuals to confront life's hurdles with heightened ease and resilience.

To harness nidra meditation for mental clarity and focus, seek out a tranquil and cozy space where you can recline and unwind. Close your eyes and embark on a journey guided by meditation, which navigates through relaxation techniques including body scanning, breath awareness, and visualization.

During nidra meditation, concentrate on relinquishing tension and surrendering to deep relaxation. While observing any arising thoughts or distractions, gently release them, redirecting your attention to the present moment. By nurturing a sanctuary of inner peace and tranquility through nidra meditation, mental clarity and focus flourish, fostering a profound sense of well-being and harmony.

In essence, nidra meditation stands as a potent practice for enhancing mental clarity and focus. Through the conduit of deep relaxation and guided meditation, it facilitates a harmonious interplay between mind and body, fostering heightened awareness and inner serenity.

By integrating nidra meditation into your daily regimen, you can cultivate a heightened ability to remain grounded and focused in the present moment, while concurrently diminishing stress, anxiety, and enhancing overall well-being. Embrace nidra meditation as a cornerstone of your routine, and unlock its transformative potential firsthand.

Chapter 10: Cultivating Compassion and Love

Nidra Yoga, also referred to as Yoga Nidra or Yogic Sleep, harnesses the potent blend of deep relaxation and mindfulness strategies to nurture compassion and love within individuals.

This ancient discipline, cherished for centuries, serves as a profound avenue for nurturing physical, mental, and emotional well-being. Its recent surge in popularity stems from its efficacy in alleviating stress, anxiety, and fostering overall health.

In the serene ambience of a Nidra Yoga session, participants recline comfortably with closed eyes as a skilled instructor orchestrates a journey through relaxation and visualization techniques.

Through rhythmic breathing, heightened body awareness, and focused mental engagement, practitioners traverse into a state akin to slumber yet maintain full consciousness.

A hallmark benefit of Nidra Yoga lies in its capacity to foster compassion and love, both inwardly and outwardly. By quieting the mind and liberating the body from tension, individuals unveil their authentic selves, tapping into an inherent wellspring of inner peace and love.

Within the sanctuary of Nidra Yoga, negative thoughts and emotions dissipate, supplanted by affirmations and intentions steeped in self-love and compassion. By nurturing acceptance and forgiveness towards oneself and others, practitioners forge a compassionate ethos that transcends the confines of the mat, permeating their daily interactions.

Moreover, Nidra Yoga fosters a profound sense of interconnectedness with all living beings, nurturing boundless compassion and empathy. By acknowledging the intrinsic value of each individual, practitioners cultivate a profound sense of unity that transcends societal divisions, fostering love and compassion towards all.

In addition to fostering compassion and love, Nidra Yoga offers a diverse array of physical and mental health benefits. This practice has been scientifically proven to alleviate stress, anxiety, and depression, enhance sleep quality, fortify immune function, and elevate overall well-being. Regular engagement with Nidra Yoga facilitates deeper relaxation, inner serenity, and emotional equilibrium.

Embarking on a journey with Nidra Yoga necessitates finding a proficient instructor who can adeptly steer you through the practice while imparting profound insights into its principles and methodologies.

Many yoga studios and wellness establishments provide Nidra Yoga classes, supplemented by a plethora of online resources and guided meditations to initiate your journey.

Within the confines of a typical Nidra Yoga session, participants are led through a sequence of relaxation techniques geared towards dissipating bodily tension, quieting the mind, and fostering inner tranquility. The instructor may orchestrate a comprehensive body scan, guiding you to each bodily region to consciously unwind, accompanied by guided visualizations and affirmations aimed at nurturing self-compassion and affection towards others.

As you persist in your Nidra Yoga practice, you may observe a transformative shift in your mindset and worldview. Gradually, you may find yourself embracing a more compassionate stance towards yourself and others, basking in heightened levels of inner peace and fulfillment. Through the cultivation of compassion and love within the realm of Nidra Yoga, you can sculpt a life characterized by harmony, gratitude, and profound connections.

In summary, Nidra Yoga stands as a potent method for nurturing compassion and love within oneself and towards others. Through the practice of profound relaxation and mindfulness, individuals can access an innate reservoir of inner peace and love, fostering the development of a compassionate mindset that transcends the confines of the yoga mat and permeates everyday life.

If you seek to alleviate stress, anxiety, and elevate your overall well-being, integrating Nidra Yoga into your daily regimen can unveil the transformative potential of compassion and love.

Nidra Meditation for Emotional Balance

Nidra meditation, often referred to as yogic sleep, stands as a potent tool for restoring emotional equilibrium and nurturing overall well-being. Rooted in ancient practices, this technique combines deep relaxation with guided imagery to quiet the mind, alleviate stress, and foster an inner sense of tranquility.

In the modern hustle and bustle, maintaining emotional balance is paramount for both mental and physical health. Amidst life's complexities, the onslaught of stress, anxiety, and negative emotions can easily overwhelm us. This is precisely where nidra meditation proves invaluable.

The essence of nidra meditation lies in guiding practitioners into a profound state of relaxation akin to the threshold between wakefulness and sleep. Within this serene space, the mind sheds its incessant chatter and concerns, paving the way for a profound sense of peace and clarity.

A cornerstone benefit of nidra meditation is its capacity to facilitate the release of pent-up emotions and stress entrenched within the body.

Emotions like anger, fear, or sorrow can manifest as physical tension, disrupting our well-being. Through nidra meditation, we gently untangle these emotional knots, ushering in a renewed sense of emotional equilibrium.

Moreover, nidra meditation serves as a gateway to mindfulness and self-awareness. By attuning ourselves to thoughts, emotions, and bodily sensations during the practice, we deepen our understanding of our inner landscape.

This heightened self-awareness empowers us to make conscious choices, establish healthy boundaries, and navigate life's complexities with grace and resilience.

To embark on a journey of emotional balance through nidra meditation, carve out a serene sanctuary where you can recline and unwind. Create a cocoon of comfort with supportive cushions for your head and neck, and perhaps an eye pillow to shield against any intrusive light. With eyes closed, initiate your practice by drawing deep breaths to anchor yourself in the present moment.

Shift your focus inward, starting from the tips of your toes and ascending through your legs, torso, arms, and finally to your head. As you traverse this internal landscape, attune yourself to any pockets of tension or discomfort, visualizing them dissolving with each exhalation. Surrender to a profound sense of relaxation, relinquishing any stray thoughts or distractions that may arise.

Once enveloped in a state of profound tranquility, summon forth a vision of serenity within your mind's eye. Whether it's a tranquil beach, a lush forest, or a majestic mountaintop, immerse yourself fully in this tranquil sanctuary. Feel the warmth of the sun caressing your skin, the gentle breeze soothing your senses, and the symphony of nature enveloping you in its embrace.

With each inhalation and exhalation, deepen your connection to this idyllic setting, allowing its essence to permeate every fiber of your being.

Notice the subtle shifts within your body, as relaxation and peace intertwine to foster a newfound emotional equilibrium. Bask in this state of profound serenity for as long as you desire, savoring the transformative effects of nidra meditation.

As you gently transition back to wakefulness, gradually reintegrate your awareness with your physical body. Gradually awaken your extremities with gentle movements, allowing your fingers and toes to wiggle and your limbs to stretch.

Take a series of deliberate breaths to rekindle your senses, grounding yourself in the present moment as you emerge from your meditative cocoon, refreshed and rejuvenated.

As you gently reopen your eyes, take a moment to introspect, observing any subtle shifts in your emotional landscape or overall sense of well-being.

Integrating nidra meditation into your daily regimen serves as a potent tool for fostering emotional equilibrium and resilience amidst life's trials. Through the intentional act of unwinding, shedding stress, and reconnecting with your inner essence, you sow the seeds of tranquility and harmony that transcend into every facet of existence.

Beyond the practice of nidra meditation, there exist myriad strategies to fortify emotional balance and well-being. Regular physical activity, nourishing dietary choices, ample rest, and nurturing connections with loved ones stand as pillars in sustaining emotional health. Seeking therapy, engaging in support networks, and embracing self-care rituals such as journaling, artistic expression, or music serve as invaluable avenues for processing emotions and bolstering resilience.

Embrace the understanding that emotional equilibrium is a dynamic journey, marked by its ebbs and flows. By weaving nidra meditation and complementary practices into the fabric of your daily routine, you cultivate an inner sanctuary of serenity and fortitude.

 Embrace the transformative potential of nidra meditation for emotional equilibrium, and embark on a journey towards holistic well-being that empowers you to navigate life's challenges with grace and resilience.

A Practice of Self-Care and Self-Love

Nidra Yoga, also recognized as Yoga Nidra or Yogic Sleep, stands as a potent modality fostering deep relaxation, self-nourishment, and self-compassion. Rooted in antiquity, this practice has traversed generations, championing holistic well-being across physical, mental, and emotional spheres.

Let's embark on an exploration of Nidra Yoga, unraveling its merits, techniques, and its potential to enrich one's overall life experience.

Understanding Nidra Yoga:

Nidra Yoga constitutes a guided meditation conducted in a reclined position conducive to relaxation. Stemming from the Sanskrit term "Nidra," meaning sleep, it earns the epithet "yogic sleep" owing to its capacity to induce a profound relaxation akin to slumber.

Yet, distinct from ordinary sleep, Nidra Yoga is a conscious endeavor, empowering practitioners to retain full awareness and presence throughout the session.

Within a Nidra Yoga session, a skilled facilitator guides participants through a series of visualizations, body scans, and breathwork exercises. Commencing with relaxation techniques to soothe the mind and body, the practice progresses with directives aimed at ushering individuals into a state of profound relaxation. The session culminates in a phase of reflection and assimilation, enabling participants to integrate the practice's benefits into their daily lives.

Benefits of Nidra Yoga:

Nidra Yoga extends a plethora of advantages encompassing physical and mental well-being. Some pivotal benefits of Nidra Yoga encompass:

1. Stress Reduction: Nidra Yoga serves as an effective ally in alleviating stress and anxiety. By eliciting the body's relaxation response, the practice aids in diminishing cortisol levels, fostering tranquility, and fortifying a sense of equilibrium.

2. Enhanced Sleep Quality: Nidra Yoga empowers individuals to augment the quality of their sleep. Through the cultivation of relaxation techniques and deep breathing practices, practitioners engender an ambiance of serenity conducive to effortless onset of sleep and sustained restfulness throughout the night.

1. Deepened Self-Awareness: Nidra Yoga serves as a pathway to fostering profound self-awareness and introspection. Within the nurturing confines of the practice, individuals are encouraged to delve into their thoughts, emotions, and convictions, fostering a deeper comprehension of the self and fostering personal evolution.

2. Heightened Mindfulness: Through Nidra Yoga, individuals embark on a journey toward cultivating

mindfulness, the art of embracing the present moment fully. By anchoring their attention to bodily sensations, breath, and the present instant, practitioners nurture an elevated awareness and gratitude for the here and now.

3. Emotional Restoration: Nidra Yoga emerges as a potent instrument for emotional healing and self-compassion. Providing a safe haven for individuals to explore their emotional landscape, the practice facilitates the processing and release of pent-up emotions, traumas, and negative thought patterns.

Practicing Nidra Yoga:

To embark on a Nidra Yoga journey, carve out a tranquil space where interruptions are minimized, and you can recline undisturbed. Utilize a yoga mat, blanket, or any supportive surface conducive to complete relaxation. Consider employing a pillow or bolster to cradle your head and neck, and an eye pillow or cloth to shield your eyes from external light.

As you settle into your chosen space, initiate your Nidra Yoga practice by following these steps:

1. Establish an Intention: Begin by setting an intention for your practice, a guiding beacon that aligns with your aspirations. This intention could revolve around reducing stress, fostering restful sleep, or nurturing self-compassion.
2. Relax the Body: Take several deep breaths to initiate a sense of serenity within your mind and body. Gradually, release tension from each body part, commencing from

the toes and ascending to the crown of the head. You may achieve this by alternately tensing and releasing muscle groups or simply directing your focus to each body part, allowing it to unwind fully.

1. Center on the Breath: After attaining a state of physical relaxation, shift your focus to your breath. Observe the rhythm of each inhalation and exhalation, allowing yourself to immerse in the sensation. Aim to elongate and regulate your breath, fostering a profound sense of tranquility and calmness.

2. Immerse in Guided Imagery: Within the realm of Nidra Yoga, surrender to the guidance of a teacher or facilitator who will lead you through a series of vivid visualizations.

These mental journeys may transport you to serene landscapes, bathe you in healing light, or envelop you in a cocoon of inner peace and serenity.

3. Contemplate and Integrate: As your practice draws to a close, embrace a moment of reflection. Tune into the shifts occurring within your body, mind, and emotions. Acknowledge any transformations experienced during the session and contemplate how you can carry the essence of your practice into your daily life, fostering a harmonious integration of its benefits.

Chapter 11: Nidra Meditation for Physical Healing and Wellbeing

Nidra meditation, or Yoga Nidra, stands as a potent practice renowned for fostering physical healing and holistic wellness. Rooted in ancient wisdom, this technique guides individuals into a state of profound relaxation akin to sleep, leveraging guided relaxation and visualization.

In the realm of physical healing, Nidra meditation capitalizes on the body's innate capacity to self-heal during deep relaxation. In moments of stress or anxiety, the release of stress hormones can detrimentally impact the immune system and overall health. Through Nidra meditation, practitioners can trigger the body's relaxation response, curbing stress hormones and facilitating healing processes.

A pivotal benefit of Nidra meditation lies in its capacity to alleviate inflammation within the body. Chronic inflammation, associated with various health conditions like heart disease and arthritis, poses significant health risks. By delving into deep relaxation through Nidra meditation, practitioners can mitigate inflammation, fostering internal healing.

Moreover, Nidra meditation plays a pivotal role in enhancing sleep quality, a cornerstone of physical healing and wellness. Sleep deprivation impedes the body's ability to repair and rejuvenate itself. By integrating Nidra meditation into bedtime rituals, individuals can soothe their minds and bodies, facilitating easier sleep initiation and maintenance.

Beyond physical healing, Nidra meditation extends its benefits to overall well-being. By mitigating stress and inducing relaxation, this practice uplifts mood, boosts energy levels, and sharpens mental clarity. Such holistic effects culminate in a profound sense of well-being and an elevated quality of life.

To embark on Nidra meditation for physical healing and well-being, carve out a serene sanctuary where you can recline undisturbed. Close your eyes and commence with a series of deep breaths, allowing the body and mind to unwind.

 Begin the journey by directing attention to each segment of the body, commencing from the toes and ascending to the crown. With each focal point, envision a gradual release, as if weightless serenity envelops each limb. With each exhalation, surrender any tension or discomfort.

Transition into a tranquil vista within the mind's eye, perhaps a tranquil beach or a verdant forest. Envision yourself nestled within this sanctuary, engulfed in profound tranquility and serenity. Surrender fully to this mental landscape, relinquishing any remnants of anxiety or strain.

In the course of your Nidra meditation, you may perceive subtle physical sensations—a gentle tingling, a comforting warmth. These sensations signal the body's descent into profound relaxation, heralding the potential for healing and well-being.

Integrating Nidra meditation into your daily regimen holds the potential to catalyze remarkable shifts in physical health and overall well-being. Through deliberate relaxation and attunement with the body, you nurture healing, alleviate stress, and elevate life's quality. Dedicate yourself to the practice of Nidra meditation consistently to unlock its transformative benefits.

In summation, Nidra meditation emerges as a potent instrument for physical rejuvenation and holistic well-being. By delving into a realm of profound relaxation through guided imagery and relaxation, we instigate healing processes, mitigate stress, and enhance sleep. Infuse Nidra meditation into your daily rituals to unlock the entirety of its ancient wisdom and benefits.

A Path to Forgiveness
and Acceptance

Nidra Yoga, known as Yoga Nidra or Yogic Sleep, serves as a potent avenue for individuals seeking forgiveness and acceptance in their lives. Rooted deeply in Vedic teachings, this ancient yoga form has long been revered for its capacity to induce relaxation, alleviate stress, and foster inner tranquility.

Central to Nidra Yoga is a guided meditation journey, guiding practitioners into a profound state of relaxation akin to the pre-sleep consciousness.

Within this realm, individuals gain access to their subconscious mind, facilitating the exploration and resolution of unresolved emotions or traumas hindering forgiveness and acceptance.

A fundamental benefit of Nidra Yoga lies in its capacity to liberate individuals from negative emotions, fostering compassion towards oneself and others. By immersing in deep relaxation, practitioners relinquish past burdens, anchoring themselves in the present to extend forgiveness for past transgressions.

Beyond forgiveness, Nidra Yoga nurtures the cultivation of self-acceptance and acceptance of circumstances. Through mindfulness and present moment awareness, individuals embrace realities without judgment or resistance, offering solace to those grappling with guilt, shame, or self-doubt.

Nidra Yoga stands as an inclusive practice, welcoming individuals of all ages and fitness levels. Unlike conventional yoga practices that involve physical postures, Nidra Yoga unfolds entirely in a comfortable reclined position, catering to those with physical constraints or injuries.

Commencing a Nidra Yoga practice is simple, requiring only a quiet, cozy space where individuals can recline and engage with guided meditation. Typically, sessions commence with a comprehensive body scan, guiding practitioners to unwind each body part from head to toe.

This process aids in the release of tension, priming the body for profound relaxation.

Following the body scan, individuals embark on a journey through guided visualizations and affirmations tailored to foster forgiveness and acceptance. These practices may involve envisioning tranquil landscapes, reciting positive affirmations, or nurturing feelings of self-love and empathy towards oneself and others.

Throughout the session, individuals are urged to relinquish negative thoughts and emotions, observing them without judgment. This fosters a sense of detachment, enabling individuals to perceive their thoughts and emotions more clearly and navigate them in a constructive manner.

With continued engagement in Nidra Yoga, individuals often experience a shift in mindset, embracing heightened peace and acceptance in their lives. Regular practice fosters a deeper sense of forgiveness towards oneself and others, empowering individuals to release past grievances and embrace newfound freedom and joy.

In addition to fostering forgiveness and acceptance, Nidra Yoga offers a plethora of benefits for both the mind and body, including:

- Stress Reduction: Nidra Yoga soothes the nervous system, alleviating stress and promoting overall relaxation and well-being.

- Improved Sleep: By inducing deep relaxation, Nidra Yoga enhances sleep quality, aiding individuals in overcoming insomnia and sleep disturbances.

- Enhanced Creativity: Nidra Yoga unlocks the subconscious mind, igniting creativity and inspiring innovation.

- Increased Focus and Concentration: Through mindfulness practices, individuals sharpen their focus and concentration skills.

- Emotional Healing: Nidra Yoga facilitates the processing of unresolved emotions and traumas, fostering emotional resilience and well-being.

In summary, Nidra Yoga stands as a potent practice for nurturing forgiveness and acceptance. By delving into deep relaxation and addressing unresolved emotions, individuals cultivate compassion towards themselves and others, paving the path for inner peace and liberation.

For those intrigued by Nidra Yoga, seeking out a qualified instructor or attending a class is recommended. With dedication to regular practice, the transformative potential of Nidra Yoga unfolds, facilitating forgiveness and acceptance in one's life.

Nidra Meditation for Inner Strength and Resilience

Nidra meditation stands as a potent method for nurturing inner fortitude and resilience. Also recognized as Yoga Nidra, this guided relaxation practice facilitates deep relaxation while maintaining consciousness and awareness.

Through Nidra meditation, you can tap into your inner reservoirs and fortify the resilience necessary for gracefully navigating life's trials.

This practice proves particularly adept at fostering inner strength and resilience by granting access to the subconscious mind, where deep-seated fears and insecurities reside. By bringing these inner obstacles to light and acknowledging them, you initiate their release and cultivate an indomitable inner strength.

A fundamental advantage of Nidra meditation lies in its capacity to liberate you from negative thought patterns and constraining beliefs that hinder progress.

Immersed in deep relaxation, you gain access to the subconscious, enabling the reprogramming of it with positive affirmations and intentions conducive to personal growth.

With continued practice, you shed outdated patterns and beliefs, replacing them with an inner fortitude that empowers you to confront life's adversities with conviction and bravery.

Beyond its role in releasing negative thought patterns and limiting beliefs, Nidra meditation offers a sanctuary for nurturing inner peace and tranquility, essential during times of stress and adversity.

Delving into a state of profound relaxation enables the mind to quieten, fostering a connection with an inner serenity always accessible, irrespective of external challenges.

This reservoir of inner peace becomes a wellspring of resilience, empowering individuals to gracefully navigate life's fluctuations.

Moreover, Nidra meditation serves as a conduit for accessing inner wisdom and intuition. Immersed in deep relaxation, individuals unlock the gates to their subconscious, tapping into the wealth of wisdom within.

This inner guidance illuminates the path forward, aiding in decision-making aligned with one's highest good and providing clarity and confidence amidst life's trials. Through cultivating this profound connection with inner wisdom and intuition, Nidra meditation lays the foundation for resilience in confronting obstacles.

Furthermore, Nidra meditation fosters the cultivation of self-love and self-compassion, pillars of support in challenging times.

Entering a state of profound relaxation facilitates a connection with an unwavering sense of love and acceptance towards oneself, regardless of circumstances. This reservoir of self-love and compassion equips individuals with the resilience necessary to face life's tribulations with kindness and understanding towards oneself, enabling a graceful rebound from setbacks and failures.

To engage in Nidra meditation for inner strength and resilience, seek out a serene and comfortable space where you can recline and unwind.

Close your eyes and initiate a sequence of deep, soothing breaths, allowing yourself to drift into profound relaxation. Employ a guided meditation or visualization to facilitate this journey inward and access your inner reservoirs of strength.

With each Nidra meditation session, witness the gradual amplification of your inner fortitude and resilience. By tapping into your inner wellsprings and nurturing feelings of inner peace, self-love, and self-compassion, you equip yourself with the resilience necessary to confront life's trials with poise and grace. Remember, resilience isn't about evading adversity, but rather about rebounding from setbacks and failures with unwavering resolve and bravery.

In essence, Nidra meditation stands as a potent tool for fortifying inner strength and resilience. Through the gateway of deep relaxation, you shed limiting beliefs and dispel negative thought patterns.

You forge a connection with inner tranquility and wisdom, while fostering self-love and compassion. With dedicated practice, you cultivate the resilience essential for traversing life's vicissitudes with resilience and emerging from challenges stronger and more resilient than before.

Chapter 12: A Practice of Gratitude and Joy

Nidra Yoga, or Yoga Nidra, stands as a potent fusion of relaxation techniques, mindfulness, and meditation, offering a pathway to profound tranquility and inner harmony.

This practice is a gateway to deep relaxation, rejuvenation, and a profound sense of inner peace. Rooted in gratitude and joy, Nidra Yoga facilitates a profound connection with oneself, nurturing gratitude for the present moment.

Described as a guided meditation practiced in a supine position, Nidra Yoga gently guides participants through a series of relaxation methods to alleviate tension and stress from both body and mind.

Commencing with a thorough body scan, practitioners focus on each part of their body, consciously unwinding and releasing tension. This heightened awareness allows for the identification and subsequent release of areas of discomfort or strain.

Continuing the practice, individuals are led through visualizations and affirmations aimed at fostering gratitude and joy. These mental images may transport one to bask in the glow of a warm, golden light or immerse in the tranquility of a serene natural landscape. Affirmations, centered on nurturing sentiments of gratitude, joy, and abundance, further cultivate an atmosphere of positivity.

Central to Nidra Yoga is the concept of sankalpa, or intention setting. Throughout the session, practitioners are encouraged to establish a positive intention or affirmation. This sankalpa serves as a guiding light, fostering the cultivation of desired qualities such as gratitude, joy, peace, or abundance. Through the repetition of this intention during the practice, seeds of positive transformation are sown within the subconscious mind.

Nidra Yoga stands as a practice accessible to all, regardless of age or fitness level, offering gentle yet profound benefits. It extends its embrace to anyone seeking respite from the hustle of daily life, especially those yearning to alleviate stress, enhance sleep quality, and nurture inner peace and well-being.

At its core, Nidra Yoga provides a sanctuary for individuals to pause amidst life's whirlwind, to breathe, and to forge deeper connections with themselves. In a world where speed is revered, this practice offers a sanctuary for stillness, a haven for inner exploration. Regular engagement with Nidra Yoga promises a reduction in stress levels, an enhancement in sleep quality, and a blossoming of gratitude and joy.

Moreover, Nidra Yoga serves as a gateway to mindfulness and presence in everyday existence. Through its gentle guidance, practitioners are encouraged to immerse themselves fully in the present moment, shedding judgment and attachment to fleeting thoughts and emotions.

This mindful awareness, honed through Nidra Yoga, equips individuals with the resilience to navigate life's undulating terrain with grace and equanimity.

Beyond its tangible physical and mental rewards, Nidra Yoga fosters a profound sense of gratitude and joy. Through consistent practice, participants awaken to the abundance and blessings that surround them, fostering a shift from scarcity to appreciation.

 This transformation in perspective ignites a radiant sense of fulfillment and contentment, illuminating the path to inner joy and harmony.

In essence, Nidra Yoga emerges as a potent ally in the pursuit of well-being, offering solace, serenity, and a pathway to gratitude and joy. Whether one is a novice or a seasoned practitioner, the transformative potential of Nidra Yoga beckons, promising enrichment and a deepening of the journey towards inner flourishing.

Nidra Meditation for
Self-Discovery and Growth

Nidra meditation, also known as yogic sleep, stands as a potent practice for delving into the subconscious realms and unlocking one's innate potential for self-discovery and personal evolution.

Rooted in ancient wisdom, this technique has traversed centuries, serving as a conduit for relaxation, stress reduction, and holistic well-being.

Within this discourse, we delve into the profound benefits nidra meditation offers for self-discovery and growth, alongside a detailed roadmap for seamlessly integrating this practice into your daily regimen.

What is Nidra Meditation?

Nidra meditation unfolds as a guided journey typically undertaken in a reclined, comfortable posture. With its Sanskrit origins translating to "sleep," nidra meditation is aptly named, for it facilitates a profound state of relaxation akin to slumber.

Through a series of guided visualizations, body scans, and breathwork, practitioners are ushered into a sanctuary of tranquility, both in body and mind.

Diverging from conventional meditation approaches that demand singular focus on a chosen anchor, such as the breath or a mantra, nidra meditation offers a gateway to deep relaxation.

Here, practitioners venture beyond the surface, delving into the recesses of the subconscious mind to navigate inner landscapes of thoughts and emotions. Particularly suited for those grappling with traditional meditation methods or battling mental chatter, nidra meditation offers an accessible pathway to inner exploration.

Benefits of Nidra Meditation for Self-Discovery and Growth

Nidra meditation unfolds a tapestry of benefits conducive to self-discovery and personal growth:

1. Stress Reduction: Nidra meditation emerges as a formidable ally in the battle against stress. By surrendering to deep relaxation, practitioners untether from tension, fostering a tranquil state of mind conducive to inner peace and holistic well-being.

2. Heightened Self-Awareness: Nidra meditation serves as a portal to the subconscious realms, inviting individuals to traverse the labyrinth of inner thoughts and emotions. Through this profound introspection, practitioners glean insights into their psyche, fostering heightened self-awareness and catalyzing personal growth.

3. Emotional Healing: Nidra meditation emerges as a potent instrument for navigating and releasing pent-up emotions. Within the nurturing cocoon of guided exploration, individuals traverse their inner landscape, finding solace in confronting emotional wounds and nurturing a newfound sense of emotional equilibrium.

4. Improved Sleep: Nidra meditation serves as a reliable ally in the pursuit of quality sleep and restorative rest. By ushering practitioners into realms of deep relaxation, this practice lays the foundation for seamless entry into sleep, fostering a night of undisturbed slumber.

5. Enhanced Creativity: Nidra meditation acts as a conduit for unlocking the reservoirs of creative potential within. By quieting the mind and delving into the subconscious, practitioners unearth a wealth of novel ideas and insights, fueling the flames of inspiration.

6. Spiritual Growth: Nidra meditation stands as a sacred vessel for spiritual deepening and communion with the divine. Through the gateway of deep relaxation, practitioners forge connections with their spiritual essence, fostering a profound sense of union with the transcendent.

How to Practice Nidra Meditation for Self-Discovery and Growth

Embark on your journey of self-discovery and personal growth through nidra meditation with these foundational steps:

1. Find a Serene Sanctuary: Seek out a tranquil and cozy space where you can recline without disruption. Lay down on a soft surface, such as a yoga mat or blanket, and support your head with a cushion for optimal comfort.

2. Set Your Intention: Prior to commencing your practice, anchor your meditation with a clear intention. Whether it's a quest for self-discovery, personal evolution, or emotional healing, articulate your purpose and infuse it into your practice with intentionality.

1. Engage with Guided Meditation: Begin your nidra meditation journey by immersing yourself in a guided session. These sessions offer structured visualizations, body scans, and breathing exercises. Explore the plethora of guided nidra meditations available online or through meditation apps to enrich your practice.

2. Unwind Your Body: As you recline in a comfortable position, initiate the relaxation process by indulging in a few deep breaths. Purposefully release tension from your muscles, starting from your feet and gradually ascending to your head. Permit each part of your body to surrender entirely to relaxation.

3. Center on Your Breath: While unwinding your body, channel your focus towards your breath. Allow it to adopt a rhythm that is unhurried and steady. Tune into the gentle ebb and flow of your chest and abdomen with each inhalation and exhalation, guiding yourself towards profound relaxation.

4. Delve into Your Inner Realm: Amidst your state of relaxation, grant your mind the liberty to wander and delve into the recesses of your inner world. Observe any thoughts or emotions that surface without passing judgment. Permit yourself to fully embrace and experience them.

A Journey to Inner Wisdom

Nidra Yoga, also referred to as Yoga Nidra or Yogic Sleep, is a potent fusion of profound relaxation and meditation, serving as a gateway for individuals to delve into their inner depths and undergo deep healing.

This ancient discipline, cherished for centuries, stands as a pillar of holistic well-being, nurturing the physical, mental, and emotional realms. In recent times, it has surged in popularity as a transformative tool for stress alleviation and personal evolution.

Nidra Yoga unfolds as a state of conscious slumber, wherein practitioners are gently guided into a profound relaxation while maintaining awareness of their surroundings.

Within this serene sanctuary of tranquility, the mind ascends to a heightened state of consciousness, where entrenched beliefs and emotions find liberation.

 Through the sacred practice of Nidra Yoga, individuals forge a connection with their inner wisdom, unraveling the mysteries of their true essence and paving the path towards living authentically in harmony with their highest self.

The journey of Nidra Yoga commences with a guided relaxation ritual, steering practitioners through soothing body scans and rhythmic breathwork to shed layers of tension. As the body surrenders to tranquility, the mind becomes a receptive vessel, ushering the practitioner into a realm of profound relaxation and meditative introspection.

Amidst the Nidra Yoga voyage, participants embark on a voyage of visualizations and affirmations meticulously crafted to unlock their inner sanctum and tap into the depths of their subconscious.

By anchoring their focus on specific intentions or aspirations, individuals sow the seeds of positive transformation within their subconscious domain, dismantling the shackles of limiting beliefs and patterns that hinder their progress.

Nidra Yoga holds a remarkable capacity to facilitate profound healing across the physical, mental, and emotional spectrums. Immersed in a state of deep relaxation, the body sheds tension and stress, fostering physical renewal and vitality.

Research underscores Nidra Yoga's efficacy in alleviating symptoms of anxiety, depression, and insomnia, offering solace to those grappling with chronic pain and illness.

On the cognitive front, Nidra Yoga serves as a beacon of clarity, enabling individuals to navigate the labyrinth of their thoughts and emotions.

This introspective voyage aids in shedding negative patterns and beliefs, paving the way for transformative growth. By delving into their inner reservoirs of wisdom, practitioners unearth profound insights into their essence, propelling them towards positive life shifts.

Emotionally, Nidra Yoga acts as a catalyst for releasing pent-up emotions and trauma, facilitating profound healing and fostering forward momentum with grace.

Through communion with their inner selves, individuals cultivate an oasis of inner peace and well-being, capable of catalyzing profound life transformations.

Beyond its healing virtues, Nidra Yoga emerges as a potent tool for personal evolution and spiritual ascension. By forging a connection with their inner wisdom, practitioners gain clarity regarding their life's purpose and trajectory, guiding them towards decisions aligned with their highest selves.

 Nidra Yoga empowers individuals to harness their intuition and creativity, emboldening them to tread an authentic path in harmony with their true purpose.

Nidra Yoga welcomes practitioners of all ages and fitness levels, fostering accessibility for everyone. Whether you're embarking on your yoga journey or already seasoned in the practice, Nidra Yoga beckons as a gentle yet potent avenue for relaxation, restoration, and inner connection.

Through consistent engagement, profound transformations unfold across the realms of physical, mental, and emotional well-being, nurturing a life enriched with authenticity and fulfillment.

In essence, Nidra Yoga stands as a potent conduit for delving into one's inner wisdom and nurturing profound healing. By seamlessly merging deep relaxation with meditative introspection, individuals unlock the gateways to their subconscious, illuminating insights into their essence. This journey fosters a harmonious alignment with one's truest self, catalyzing a life brimming with authenticity and purpose.

Whether the quest is for stress reduction, emotional healing, or gaining clarity in life's labyrinth, Nidra Yoga emerges as a cherished ally for personal evolution and metamorphosis. Embark on the voyage to inner wisdom today with Nidra Yoga and unravel the tapestry of profound benefits awaiting your embrace.

.

Chapter 13: Nidra Meditation for Letting Go of Past Trauma

Nidra meditation, also referred to as Yoga Nidra, stands as a potent practice empowering individuals to shed the weight of past trauma, fostering peace and healing. Rooted in deep relaxation, it emerges as a precious tool for those grappling with the lingering effects of trauma.

Exploring Nidra Meditation:

Nidra meditation unfolds as a guided practice, typically conducted in a reclined, comfortable posture. Often likened to "yogic sleep," it induces a state of profound relaxation akin to slumber while maintaining complete awareness. Guided through a series of directives, practitioners ease into a tranquil state, soothing the body, calming the mind, and traversing into profound relaxation.

The Healing Potency of Nidra Meditation for Overcoming Past Trauma:

Nidra meditation unveils a robust arsenal for navigating past trauma and embarking on the path to healing. Here's a glimpse into its transformative benefits for trauma survivors:

1. Deep Relaxation: Nidra meditation orchestrates a profound union of body and mind in deep relaxation.

This gentle immersion into tranquility becomes a sanctuary for trauma survivors, facilitating the release of pent-up tension and stress held within the body's depths.

2. Heightened Awareness: Nidra meditation serves as a beacon illuminating the inner landscape, enhancing awareness of thoughts, emotions, and bodily sensations. This heightened awareness becomes a guiding light for trauma survivors, offering a safe haven to recognize, confront, and process their experiences with compassion and understanding.

1. Restoring Harmony to the Nervous System: Trauma often leaves a lasting imprint on the nervous system, manifesting as anxiety, depression, or hypervigilance. Through Nidra meditation, individuals embark on a journey to soothe the frazzled nerves, fostering healing and restoring a sense of peace and security.

2. Breaking Free from Negative Patterns: Trauma weaves intricate webs of negative thought patterns and beliefs, ensnaring individuals in their grip. Nidra meditation serves as a beacon of liberation, guiding practitioners to identify and release these entangled patterns. With newfound clarity, they pave the way for embracing fresh, affirming perspectives.

3. Nurturing Self-Compassion: In the aftermath of trauma, individuals often find themselves adrift, disconnected from their essence and others. Nidra meditation becomes a nurturing embrace, fostering self-compassion and self-love. As they traverse the path of healing, practitioners

cultivate a profound sense of self-worth and acceptance, forging ahead with renewed vigor and grace.

How to Engage in Nidra Meditation for Releasing Past Trauma:

For those inclined to employ Nidra meditation as a catalyst for shedding past trauma, here's a roadmap to embark on this transformative journey:

1. Seek Serenity in a Tranquil Setting: Prepare a serene sanctuary for your Nidra meditation practice—a tranquil space where disturbances are but fleeting whispers. Envelop yourself in comfort, laying upon a soft surface with supportive cushions cradling your form.

2. Set Intentions with Purpose: Prior to delving into your Nidra meditation, carve a moment to set intentions that resonate with your healing journey. Whether it's releasing past trauma or fostering self-compassion, infuse your practice with intentions that reflect your aspirations for transformation.

1. Explore Guided Nidra Meditations: Dive into the wealth of guided Nidra meditation resources available online or through meditation apps. Discover a session that resonates with you, allowing the gentle guidance to lead you through the practice.

2. Tune into Body Sensations: Throughout your Nidra meditation journey, you'll encounter prompts to tune into various sensations in your body—warmth, heaviness, tingling, and more. Embrace these sensations,

surrendering to their soothing embrace as you delve deeper into relaxation.

3. Cultivate Consistency: Just like tending to a garden, the benefits of Nidra meditation blossom with regular nurturing. Aim to weave Nidra meditation seamlessly into your daily routine, whether it's dedicating a few moments each day or immersing yourself in longer sessions.

4. Practice Patience and Kindness: Healing from past trauma is a tender journey that unfolds gradually. Approach your Nidra meditation practice with patience and kindness, acknowledging the layers of healing as they unfold. Remember, each moment of practice is a step forward on your path to wholeness.

In essence, Nidra meditation offers a profound pathway to releasing past trauma and embracing healing. Through regular practice, individuals can unwind the knots of tension in their bodies, quiet the chatter of the mind, and foster self-compassion.

If you've traversed the terrain of past trauma, consider integrating Nidra meditation into your daily repertoire—a gentle yet potent ally on your healing odyssey.

A Path to Empowerment
and Liberation

Nidra Yoga, commonly referred to as Yogic Sleep, stands as a transformative practice, offering individuals pathways to empowerment and liberation.

Rooted in ancient Vedas, this profound technique merges deep relaxation with guided meditation, guiding practitioners to delve into their subconscious realms, where entrenched tensions and traumas reside.

Through Nidra Yoga's gentle embrace, individuals embark on a journey of holistic healing and evolution, spanning physical, mental, emotional, and spiritual dimensions.

With origins tracing back millennia to the sacred texts of the Vedas, Nidra Yoga was revered as a conduit for profound relaxation and inner renewal, granting seekers access to elevated states of consciousness and intimate communion with their inner selves.

In contemporary times, the practice has garnered widespread acclaim in the Western world, celebrated as a potent remedy for stress alleviation, restoration, and personal metamorphosis.

Central to the philosophy of Nidra Yoga lies the principle of "Sankalpa," or intention. Prior to embarking on a Nidra Yoga session, practitioners are encouraged to articulate a positive intention or affirmation, serving as a luminous beacon guiding their practice. This intention acts as a steadfast ally, anchoring individuals to their aspirations and propelling them forward on their journey of growth and fulfillment.

In the tranquil sanctuary of a Nidra Yoga session, participants recline in comfort, attuning their senses to the soothing cadence of a guided meditation led by a seasoned instructor.

Through a harmonious blend of breathwork, body scanning, and visualization, practitioners surrender to the gentle currents of relaxation, traversing realms of serenity and introspection. In this sacred space, tensions dissolve, giving rise to sensations of weightlessness and expansiveness, while a profound sense of peace and tranquility permeates the soul.

As practitioners delve deeper into Nidra Yoga, they embark on a journey into their subconscious realms, uncovering hidden beliefs, emotions, and memories that may hinder their progress.

By illuminating these unconscious patterns, individuals initiate a process of healing, shedding light on old wounds, traumas, and limiting beliefs. This process of introspection and self-discovery serves as a catalyst for personal growth and transformation, paving the way for profound inner change.

Nidra Yoga serves as a conduit for tapping into inner wisdom and intuition, offering practitioners clarity and insight into their lives and relationships.

Through communion with their higher selves, individuals gain access to a deeper sense of purpose and meaning, fostering greater fulfillment and joy across all facets of existence.

Amidst the chaos of modern life, Nidra Yoga emerges as a potent remedy for stress relief and relaxation. In a world saturated with stressors and anxiety, regular practice of Nidra Yoga enables individuals to attain deep relaxation, liberating the body and mind from tension. This newfound sense of calm and inner peace becomes a sanctuary amidst life's tumultuous currents.

Beyond its tangible benefits, Nidra Yoga holds the power to catalyze spiritual growth and evolution. By forging a connection with the divine essence within, practitioners experience unity with the cosmos, nurturing profound feelings of peace, love, and compassion.

Through the transformative practice of Nidra Yoga, individuals cultivate a profound bond with their higher selves and the universe, ushering in a profound sense of empowerment and liberation.

In essence, Nidra Yoga serves as a transformative journey towards empowerment and liberation across all dimensions of existence. Through its profound techniques of delving into the subconscious, unwinding deep-seated tensions and traumas, and fostering a connection with inner wisdom and intuition, individuals unlock avenues for profound healing and metamorphosis.

Whether the aim is to alleviate stress, enhance well-being, or enrich spiritual exploration, Nidra Yoga presents a universal pathway to empowerment and liberation, accessible to all who seek it.

Nidra Meditation for Transforming Pain into Peace

Nidra meditation, also referred to as yoga nidra or yogic sleep, serves as a potent practice capable of transmuting pain into serenity. Rooted in ancient wisdom, this technique combines profound relaxation and mindfulness to enable individuals to delve into their subconscious and release negative emotions and experiences.

Through regular nidra meditation, individuals can cultivate the ability to relinquish pain and suffering, paving the way for a profound inner peace and tranquility.

Pain, in its myriad forms—be it physical, emotional, or psychological—constitutes a shared human experience. Whether grappling with chronic physical discomfort, navigating the depths of loss or heartache, or confronting past traumas and adversities, pain has the capacity to ensnare and hinder our capacity for joyful living.

Nidra meditation emerges as a comprehensive approach to pain healing, addressing its underlying causes and effecting transformation at the profoundest levels of mind and body.

Central to the nidra meditation practice is the act of reclining in a comfortable position, closing the eyes, and surrendering to the guidance of a skilled instructor or pre-recorded meditation. The journey typically commences with a meticulous body scan, directing attention to each body part to induce conscious relaxation and alleviate physical tension, thus priming the body for deep relaxation.

As relaxation deepens, practitioners are led through a sequence of visualizations and affirmations meticulously crafted to access the subconscious and untangle negative emotions and beliefs.

By fostering awareness of thoughts, emotions, and bodily sensations, individuals embark on a journey of unraveling the layers of accumulated pain and suffering.

A hallmark benefit of nidra meditation lies in its capacity to foster a profound sense of inner peace and acceptance. Through immersion in deep relaxation and mindfulness, individuals cultivate the ability to observe pain without judgment or resistance, thereby facilitating its natural dissolution and transformation.

This process of surrender and release heralds a journey of liberation and empowerment, liberating individuals from the clutches of pain and ushering them into realms of profound peace and well-being.

Nidra meditation serves as a conduit for developing profound self-awareness and self-compassion, integral qualities for navigating pain and trauma. Through the cultivation of mindfulness and presence, individuals learn to observe their thoughts and emotions impartially, allowing them to ebb and flow like passing clouds in the sky.

This practice of non-attachment liberates individuals from the shackles of suffering, fostering a state of peace and equanimity amidst life's tribulations.

Beyond its emotional and psychological merits, nidra meditation yields transformative effects on the physical body. By inducing deep relaxation, the practice mitigates stress hormones, reduces blood pressure, and enhances overall health and well-being. Scientific studies attest to its capacity to fortify the immune system, ameliorate sleep quality, and alleviate symptoms of anxiety and depression.

A distinctive facet of nidra meditation lies in its ability to access the subconscious mind and engage with the body's energy centers, known as chakras.

Through targeted visualizations and affirmations, practitioners can activate and harmonize these chakras, which regulate various aspects of physical, emotional, and spiritual well-being. By fostering awareness of these energy centers and dissolving any blockages or imbalances, individuals facilitate profound healing and transformation.

For those grappling with chronic pain or trauma, nidra meditation emerges as a potent ally for healing and recovery. Through consistent and intentional practice, individuals embark on a journey of unraveling the layers of accumulated pain and suffering, cultivating an inner landscape characterized by peace and resilience.

By embracing deep relaxation and mindfulness, practitioners learn to relinquish the past, embracing the present moment with grace and compassion.

If delving into nidra meditation to transmute pain into peace intrigues you, numerous resources are available to initiate your journey.

You might opt to attend a guided nidra meditation class or workshop, listen to pre-recorded meditations online, or embark on solo practice sessions in the comfort of your home. Whichever avenue you select, maintaining an open mind and a willingness to delve into the depths of your consciousness is paramount.

In summary, nidra meditation stands as a potent practice capable of guiding individuals towards transforming pain into peace. Through fostering deep relaxation, mindfulness, and self-awareness, one can commence shedding negative emotions and beliefs that hinder progress, paving the way for profound inner tranquility and well-being.

Whether grappling with chronic physical pain, emotional trauma, or simply yearning for greater life balance and harmony, nidra meditation emerges as a valuable instrument for healing and transformation. Embrace the practice and witness firsthand its profound impact on your mind, body, and spirit.

Chapter14: Embracing the Power of Now

Nidra Yoga, or Yogic Sleep, stands as a potent practice enabling individuals to reach profound relaxation while maintaining consciousness. Often utilized as a meditative tool, it aids in tethering individuals to the present, facilitating the release of stress and tension. Its inclusive nature allows people of all ages and abilities to partake, ensuring accessibility for all.

Central to Nidra Yoga is the embrace of the power of the present moment. Anchoring oneself fully in the now entails shedding concerns about the past or future, fostering a serene and composed outlook beneficial for navigating life's hurdles.

Nidra Yoga unfolds through a series of guided meditations and visualizations, fostering bodily and mental relaxation. These techniques aid in tension and stress release, ushering practitioners into a state of profound tranquility. Consistent practice cultivates mindfulness, anchoring individuals in the present and enhancing their sense of groundedness.

Among its myriad benefits, Nidra Yoga excels in inducing deep relaxation, liberating practitioners from physical and mental strains. This proves especially advantageous for those grappling with stress, anxiety, or sleep disorders.

Moreover, Nidra Yoga nurtures self-awareness, inviting practitioners to delve into their thoughts, emotions, and physical sensations. This heightened self-awareness fosters a deeper understanding of oneself and one's needs, empowering individuals to make conscious choices in their lives.

Nidra Yoga offers a myriad of benefits, including the promotion of healing and rejuvenation. Through deep relaxation, practitioners allow their bodies and minds to rest and recharge, effectively combatting both physical and mental fatigue. This restoration leaves individuals feeling more energized and revitalized.

Moreover, Nidra Yoga facilitates not only relaxation and self-awareness but also cultivates inner peace and contentment. By relinquishing concerns about the past or future and immersing oneself in the present moment, practitioners can experience profound tranquility, enabling them to navigate life's challenges with grace and ease.

To engage in Nidra Yoga, individuals typically assume a comfortable position and partake in a guided meditation. Led by a teacher, participants undergo visualizations and affirmations crafted to foster relaxation and mindfulness. As they unwind both body and mind, they may enter a state akin to sleep, yet with heightened awareness.

Accessible to individuals of all ages and abilities, Nidra Yoga is particularly beneficial for those contending with stress, anxiety, or insomnia. Consistent practice yields deep relaxation, enhanced self-awareness, and inner peace, empowering individuals to confront life's trials with resilience.

In essence, Nidra Yoga empowers individuals to embrace the present moment. By prioritizing the here and now and relinquishing worries of yesterday and tomorrow, practitioners unlock profound relaxation, heightened self-awareness, and inner tranquility. For those seeking to nurture mindfulness and relaxation in their lives, integrating Nidra Yoga into their daily regimen holds immense promise.

Nidra Meditation for Deep Rest and Relaxation

Nidra Meditation, also referred to as Yoga Nidra, stands as a potent method for achieving profound relaxation and restoration. This guided meditation technique facilitates a state of conscious deep sleep, ushering practitioners into a realm of profound tranquility and renewal.

With roots tracing back through centuries, Nidra Meditation has served as a cornerstone for promoting holistic well-being encompassing physical, mental, and emotional realms. In this discourse, we will delve into the manifold benefits of Nidra Meditation and explore ways to seamlessly integrate it into your daily routine, offering a pathway to profound repose and relaxation.

The practice of Nidra Meditation unfolds with practitioners reclining in a comfortable position, embarking on a journey guided by meditation prompts.

Commencing with a thorough body scan, attention is directed to each bodily region, inviting the release of tension and surrender to deeper states of relaxation. Subsequently, guided visualizations and affirmations pave the path to unburdening stress and anxiety, ushering participants into a state of profound repose.

At the heart of Nidra Meditation lies its capacity to induce a state of deep relaxation akin to the restorative slumber experienced during nocturnal rest. This profound repose serves as a catalyst for bodily repair and rejuvenation, fostering optimal physical health and well-being. Robust research underscores the efficacy of Nidra Meditation in mitigating stress, anxiety, and depression, enhancing sleep quality, and bolstering the immune system.

Nidra Meditation serves as a potent tool for enhancing mental clarity and focus. By immersing yourself in deep relaxation, you can silence the chatter of the mind and release racing thoughts and concerns.

 This fosters improved concentration, memory, and cognitive function, enabling you to approach tasks with a lucid and centered mind. Moreover, Nidra Meditation unlocks your creativity and intuition, facilitating access to fresh ideas and insights.

On an emotional level, Nidra Meditation aids in shedding negative emotions and nurturing inner peace and tranquility. By relinquishing stress and anxiety, you create room for positive feelings like joy, gratitude, and love to blossom. Furthermore, Nidra Meditation fosters heightened self-awareness and self-compassion, fostering deeper connections with yourself and others.

To integrate Nidra Meditation into your daily regimen, carve out a quiet and comfortable space where you can recline undisturbed for 20-30 minutes. Whether guided by a recording or self-directed, commence by centering yourself with a few deep breaths. Then, systematically scan your body from head to toe, releasing tension and surrendering to profound relaxation.

As you immerse yourself in the practice, let go of any intrusive thoughts or distractions, anchoring your focus in the present moment. Follow the meditation's guidance, allowing yourself to sink deeper into relaxation with each breath. Envision yourself amidst a tranquil setting, reinforcing relaxation and well-being through affirmations.

Upon completion of the meditation, gradually reorient yourself to the present by gently wiggling your fingers and toes, and stretching your body. Take note of the post-meditation sensations – a sense of relaxation, rejuvenation, and inner peace. Embrace Nidra Meditation as a daily ritual or as needed, nurturing deep rest and relaxation in your life.

In essence, Nidra Meditation stands as a potent practice for profound relaxation, enriching your physical, mental, and emotional well-being. By weaving this practice into your daily routine, you unlock the potential for deep relaxation, stress reduction, enhanced sleep quality, and sharpened mental acuity. Embrace Nidra Meditation as a transformative journey toward holistic wellness.

A Comprehensive to Inner
Peace and Wellbeing

Nidra Yoga, often referred to as Yogic Sleep, stands as a transformative practice for nurturing inner peace and well-being. This ancient yoga form merges relaxation techniques with meditation to evoke a profound state of relaxation and heightened awareness.

Within this comprehensive guide, we delve into the myriad benefits of Nidra Yoga, effective practice methods, and its potential to enhance overall health and wellness.

Understanding Nidra Yoga

Nidra Yoga epitomizes a yoga discipline centered on deep relaxation and meditation. Rooted in Sanskrit, "Nidra" translates to sleep, earning it the moniker Yogic Sleep due to its ability to induce a state of profound relaxation akin to slumber. However, unlike conventional sleep, Nidra Yoga is a conscious practice that enables practitioners to maintain awareness and presence while submerged in deep relaxation.

Throughout a Nidra Yoga session, individuals are gently ushered through an array of relaxation techniques, encompassing deep breathing, body scanning, and visualization. These practices serve to alleviate bodily and mental tension, empowering individuals to relinquish stress and strain. As the session unfolds, practitioners journey into a realm of deep meditation, where they can explore their innermost thoughts and emotions within a nurturing and secure environment.

Benefits of Nidra Yoga

Nidra Yoga offers a plethora of benefits when practiced regularly. Some of these include:

1. Stress Reduction: Nidra Yoga serves as a potent stress and anxiety alleviator. By delving into deep relaxation, individuals can shed tension and quiet the mind, fostering a serene and tranquil state.

2. Improved Sleep: Nidra Yoga aids in enhancing sleep quality. By incorporating relaxation techniques before bedtime, individuals can foster a calming atmosphere conducive to easier sleep initiation and sustained rest throughout the night.

3. Increased Awareness: Nidra Yoga facilitates heightened awareness of thoughts, emotions, and physical sensations. Through mindfulness and meditation practices, individuals can nurture greater self-awareness and self-compassion.

4. Enhanced Creativity: Nidra Yoga acts as a catalyst for unlocking creative potential. By immersing in deep relaxation, individuals can access the subconscious mind, fostering exploration of novel ideas and perspectives.

5. Emotional Healing: Nidra Yoga emerges as a potent tool for emotional processing and healing. Within a safe and supportive environment, individuals can delve into inner thoughts and emotions, facilitating the release of pent-up emotions and fostering a sense of peace and healing.

How to Practice Nidra Yoga

To engage in effective Nidra Yoga practice, adhere to these guidelines:

1. Secure a serene and comfortable space devoid of distractions, where you can recline and unwind peacefully...

Here's a refreshed version of the content:

1. Find a comfortable spot, lying on your back with arms resting by your sides and legs slightly apart. Close your eyes, take a few deep breaths, and let your body and mind relax.

2. Focus on your breath, inhaling deeply and exhaling slowly. Notice how each breath fills you and empties out, grounding you in the present moment.

3. Start to scan your body from head to toe, noticing any areas of tension or discomfort. With each exhale, envision releasing any stress or tightness from these areas.

4. Continue the body scan, directing your attention to each body part individually. Picture a warm wave of relaxation washing over you as you release tension.

5. As your body relaxes, turn your focus inward to your thoughts and emotions. Allow them to arise without judgment, simply observing them as they come and go.

6. Visualize yourself in a tranquil setting, like a serene beach or a peaceful forest. Immerse yourself fully in this mental image, embracing the sights, sounds, and sensations of calmness.

7. Slowly bring yourself back to the present, wiggling your fingers and toes, and gently opening your eyes. Take a moment to reflect on your experience and notice how you feel.

Regular practice of Nidra Yoga can cultivate inner peace and well-being, reducing stress, enhancing sleep quality, and promoting overall health.

In summary, Nidra Yoga offers a potent pathway to inner tranquility and health. By merging relaxation techniques with meditation, this ancient yoga form empowers individuals to release stress, improve sleep, and elevate their well-being.

Whether you're new to yoga or a seasoned practitioner, integrating Nidra Yoga into your routine can foster a serene mindset that enriches both your practice and your daily life. Embark on your Nidra Yoga journey today and unlock the transformative potential of Yogic Sleep.

Conclusion

In the closing chapter of "Nidra Yoga Meditation: Stress Management, Mental Health, and Inner Peace," you've reached a pivotal moment in your journey towards holistic well-being. Delving deep into the transformative practices of Nidra Yoga Meditation, you've unearthed the tools needed to navigate life's twists and turns with resilience and tranquility.

Throughout this exploration, you've honed relaxation techniques, cultivated mindfulness, and strengthened your connection to the present moment. These practices have become the cornerstone of your journey towards managing stress, nurturing mental health, and fostering a sense of inner peace that radiates from within.

Beyond these pages, the essence of transformation lies within your grasp. As you step forward into each new day, carry with you the wisdom gleaned from your journey. With intention and commitment, integrate these teachings into your daily life, prioritizing self-care and embracing the principles of Nidra Yoga Meditation.

May this book serve as a beacon of guidance on your path towards wholeness and vitality. Embrace the adventure that lies ahead, trusting in your inner wisdom to illuminate the way. With the transformative power of Nidra Yoga Meditation as your guide, may you discover a life filled with enduring joy, equilibrium, and fulfillment. Your journey towards profound well-being starts now.

Biography

Introducing Elianne Hartz, a fervent advocate for holistic well-being and the creative mind behind an enlightening book centered on Nidra Yoga Meditation. Rooted in a background of mental health counseling and a profound dedication to personal growth, Elianne offers a treasure trove of expertise in stress management and mindfulness.

Harnessing years of practice as a certified yoga instructor specializing in Nidra Yoga Meditation, Elianne is on a mission to empower individuals in discovering inner harmony amid life's trials. Her approach marries ancient wisdom with contemporary insights, equipping readers with tangible tools to enrich their mental well-being and nurture tranquility in their daily lives.

Beyond her professional pursuits, Elianne finds sanctuary in the embrace of yoga nidra meditation, rejuvenating her mind, body, and soul. She champions the transformative potency of self-care, prioritizing her own vitality through regular yoga nidra sleep sessions and mindfulness rituals.

During leisure moments, Elianne can be found wandering nature's trails, immersing herself in creative endeavors like painting and writing, or simply unwinding with a captivating read. Her diverse passions echo her holistic ethos and steadfast commitment to living authentically and purposefully.

Through her book and personal odyssey, Elianne extends an invitation to embark on a voyage of self-discovery and empowerment. Together, let's traverse a path illuminated by vitality, resilience, and enduring inner peace. Join Elianne on this revelatory expedition and unlock the boundless potential of Nidra Yoga Meditation to embrace a life brimming with fulfillment.